# THE STORY OF ASTROLOGY:

## THE BELIEF IN THE STARS
## AS A FACTOR IN HUMAN PROGRESS

## MANLY PALMER HALL

COSIMO CLASSICS

NEW YORK

**The Story of Astrology: The Belief in the Stars as a Factor in Human Progress**
© 2005 Cosimo, Inc.

Cosimo, P.O. Box 416
Old Chelsea Station
New York, NY 10113-0416

or visit our website at:
www.cosimobooks.com

*The Story of Astrology: The Belief in the Stars as a Factor in Human Progress* originally published by David McKay Company in 1933 .

**Library of Congress Cataloging-in-Publication Data**
A catalog record for this book is available from the Library of Congress

Cover design by www.wiselephant.com

ISBN: 1-59605-707-6

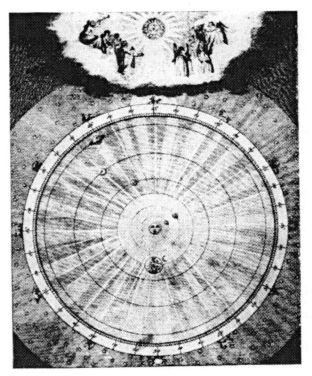

*The Harmony of the Spheres.*

# TABLE OF CONTENTS

# INTRODUCTION

*"Understand, Therefore, Concerning Astrology That It Knows the Whole Nature, Wisdom, and Science of the Stars, According As They Perfect Their Own Operation in Conception and Constitute an Animal Man. . . . But if Astrology Be Fundamentally and Properly Known, and the Nativities of Infants Be Erected Rightly According to the Mode of the Influence, Many Evils Will Be Avoided Which Would Otherwise Be Occasioned by the Unpropitious Constellations."*—PARACELSUS.

THE purpose of this small volume is to render available in compact and simple form the leading facts of astrological history. Our treatise is by no means complete—the subject is entirely too vast to be enclosed by the narrow covers of so slight a work. Yet as few historians have appeared to present the claims of the ancient science to an unbelieving world since Sir Christopher Heydon compiled his celebrated *Defense of Judicial Astrology* in 1603, it would seem that some effort in this direction is not untimely. We have gathered our data from many sources, most of which are acknowledged in the text or footnotes, and recommend that those who choose to explore more deeply into the subject should examine carefully the volumes referred to.

The notes of the present writing originally formed the basis of a lecture on *Astrological Origins* delivered before the Third Annual Convention of the National Astrological Association. The purpose of the lecture was twofold; first, to supply students of astrology with some tangible data concerning the antiquity, dignity and significance of the science; and, second, to correct miscomprehensions relating to the subject which have been deliberately promulgated by prejudiced scientists and theologians. Astrologers, especially in America, are constantly subjected to humiliating and unwarranted indignities because of their allegiance to an art, the accuracy of which has been established by several thousand years of observation and experimentation. The astrologer has been unjustifiably ridiculed by the body of the so-called learned, and is seldom if ever given a fair opportunity to explain the principles of his science. Nearly all accounts of astrology which have appeared in standard research works on science and history have been written by opponents of its principles, and when the literati are forced by the requirements of their subject matter to refer to the starry lore, they seldom fail to make some slighting and usually untruthful remark about the science, to the discredit of themselves rather than of astrology. The public is constantly warned that to believe in astrology is to be little better than mildly insane. Astronomy brands astrology as a medieval superstition peculiar to washwomen, midwives and gypsies. Depending solely upon a somewhat questionable reputation for infallibility, savants of the modern school, with one grand and impressive gesture, pronounce an anathema against all of the occult sciences and relegate astrology to limbo.

The proper end of all learning is to discover Cause. Science exists that it may glorify fact and establish truth, yet for certain reasons entirely beyond scientific control, Cause remains unknown, fact is obscure, and truth only a word. The layman seeking knowledge of the sidereal world, naturally turns to the astronomer whose self-appointed task it is to measure the immensities of space and classify the great energies that are resident therein.

If the modern astronomer solemnly announces that the heavenly bodies can produce no moral effect upon the earth, this pronouncement is regarded as scriptural in its finality. It seldom occurs to the average person that the astronomer has proved nothing by his solemn pronouncement and, if the truth were known, is not in a position to prove anything. Astrology has never been scientifically disproved, all blustering to the contrary notwithstanding.

The great Sir Isaac Newton, who combined excellence of intellect with a becoming humility, was brought to the study of astronomy by his early interest in astrology. On one occasion, when complimented upon the profundity of his erudition, Newton replied with a gentle smile, "If I appear to see farther than other men, it is because I am standing upon the shoulders of giants." We would humbly remind the modern scientist that he too is greatly indebted to the ages for that wisdom which is now his boast. The giants upon whose shoulders Newton stood were Pythagoras, Ptolemy, Copernicus, Galileo, Kepler, and Brahe. These illustrious men were all astrologers but showed none of the symptoms of that mental deterioration from which, according to modern science, all astrologers suffer.

Is it then superstition or scientific heresy to suggest that a subject, which has occupied the minds of the world's ablest thinkers for the entire period of the world's recorded history, might be worthy of a more tolerant attitude by our modern pedagogues?

We come not with old wives' tales but with a well-founded tradition, thoroughly established in the three great requisites of knowledge—authority, observation, and experimentation—which according to Lord Bacon are the proper bases for the building up of a scientific premise. To quote Lord Bacon, who states definitely that Astrology may be "more confidently" applied to Prophecy: "Predictions may be made of comets to come, which (I am inclined to think) may be foretold; of all kinds of meteors, of floods, droughts, heats, frosts, earthquakes, eruptions of water, eruptions of fire, great winds and rains, various seasons of the year, plagues, epidemic diseases, plenty and dearth of grain, wars, sedition, schisms, transmigrations of peoples, and any other or all commotions or general revolutions of things, natural as well as civil."[1]

Modern astronomy deals only with the physical composition of the cosmos. In a recent effort to justify his own existence, one astronomer wrote at considerable length to prove that without the invaluable contribution of his science our time calculations would lack precision and our trains run off schedule. (!!) Ergo, again the mountain gives birth to a mouse. Ancient astronomers, that is astrologers, were concerned primarily with the intellectual and moral energy of the universe. Materialism in the present century has perverted the application of knowledge from its legitimate ends, thus permitting so noble a science as astronomy to become a purely abstract and comparatively useless instrument which can contribute little more than tables of meaningless figures to a world bankrupt in spiritual, philosophical and ethical values. The problem as to whether space is a straight or curved extension may intrigue a small number of highly specialized minds, but the moral relationship between man and space and the place of the human soul in the harmony of the spheres is vastly more important to a world afflicted with every evil that the flesh is heir to.

[1] See *De Augmentis.*

We may be accused of writing this treatise from a bias, as, according to the present temper, criticism is the very cornerstone of scholarship, and it is the scientific fashion to open a deep argument by a wholesale castigation of antiquity, along with a fair drubbing of dissenting confreres. We ignore the slanders of these numerous sciolists who seek only evil in the opinions of other men. It is impossible to answer an attack in which no effort is made to present reasonable argument. Science does not make a case against astrology, but merely unconditionally condemns without consideration, examination or research. If our writing is devoted entirely to the defense of astrology it is because practically every available article on the subject by non-astrological (and supposedly unbiased) authors is an unqualified attack.

While criticism remains the profession of the uninformed, astrology will never lack defamers.

It is our desire to correct several glaring untruths now circulated concerning astrology. The public is assured that the old science is practically defunct, and leading educators gloss over the whole matter by referring to astrology as extinct. The facts are that astrology today has probably a greater number of advocates than ever before in its long and illustrious history. Book dealers and librarians will testify that works on this subject are in ever increasing demand and the standard of their scholarship is constantly improving. Europe, especially Germany, has become distinctly astrology-conscious, and the technical Teutonic mind is carrying on extensive and exhaustive research with extremely significant results. France and England are continuing a dignified promulgation of astrological ideas, and astrology in all its branches is sweeping over America in a wave of enthusiasm. Students of the subject in the

United States must be numbered in the tens if not hundreds of thousands and several correspondence courses on astrology are spreading the fundamentals of the science through the cities and towns of the various states. The late Evangeline Adams received over 300,000 letters a year from persons interested in astrology, and men and women in every walk of life, including not a few famous in the world of letters, have recognized both the theoretical and practical values of the science. While it is true that opponents of astrology are untiring in their efforts to discredit the whole subject, astrology goes victoriously on, enjoying the patronage of liberal minded and progressive persons in all lands.

An effort has also been made to show that astrology is irreconcilable with the religious principles which dominate so great a part of the *nominally* Christian world. Theologians have for the most part gone into partnership with their worst enemies, the materialistic scientists, in viewing astrology as the common enemy. Some centuries ago a distinguished Episcopalian clergyman, the Reverend John Butler, B. D., Rector of Litchborough, felt himelf called upon to exterminate the astrologers of England. In order to gain more information from which to distill venom, he decided to read "moderately" on the subject, when lo and behold a miracle occurred! This is best expressed in his own words:

"Myself also must needs acknowledge, that some years since, I also was one of those enemies to this noble science, who buffetted in the dark I know not what: until soberly tempted to taste a few lines reading of this subject, although it was with a serious purpose, to take up the apter occasion to throw dirt at it; yet by this means attaining to understand who it was I spoke to, it begot in me a reverence for these gray hairs, which as unjustly as ignorantly I had despised. . . . And while I study thus I find that next unto Theology, nothing leads me more near unto this sight of God, than this sacred astrological study of the great works of nature."[2]

Much of the religious inspiration of Christendom is derived from the ancient Jews and it is not amiss to realize that astrology was greatly cultivated by the wisest among the ancient Israelites; according to Heydon, even by Moses himself, who must needs have been proficient in it because he was a priest of the Egyptians. The Jewish Encyclopaedia contains the following, a typical example of the reverence with which the Biblical patriarchs administered astrological knowledge:

"Abraham, the Chaldean, bore upon his breast a large astrological tablet on which the fate of every man might be read; for which reason—according to the Haggadist—all the kings of the East and of the West congregated every morning before his door in order to seek advice."

Jewish masters in astrology were numerous. There was Kalir, Ibn Gabirol, Jacob ibn Tarik, Sahl b. Bishr al-Israeli, Andruzagar-ben Zadi Faruk, Shabbethai Donalo, Abraham b. Hiyya. Abraham ibn Ezra called astrology the sublime science. Then there was Abraham ben David of Posquieres, Judah ha-Levi, Abraham ibn Daud, Albo, Isaac Arama, Solomon b. Adret, and David Gans. Maimonides, the greatest of the Jewish philosophers, observes: "For as much as God hath created these stars and spheres to govern the world and hath set them on high and hath imparted honor unto them, and they are ministers that minister before Him, it is meet that men should laud and glorify and give them honor."

The New Schaff-Herzog Encyclopaedia of Religious
_____
[2] See *Hagiastrologia*.

Knowledge contains the following curious allusion to the birth of Christ: "The Star of the Magi (Matthew ii) was probably a conjunction, in the sign of the Fish, of Jupiter and Saturn in the year of Rome 747, a coincidence which Abar Danel states was recorded by Jewish astrologers as an indication of the Messiah." Nor should we forget Rabbi Hanina who said: "Go to the son of Levi, and tell him that the fate of the person is not decided by the constellations of the day but by those of the hour."

From these fragments it will be evident that the compilers of the Bible and the commentators thereon, together with the most learned of Israel, found no more sacrilege in astrology than did those Popes of the Christian Church who are listed in the second section of this work.

Astrology, from the time of Hippocrates, was regarded as an extremely valuable aid in the diagnosing of disease, and even at this time a number of physicians have recourse to its diagnostic aspect, usually without the knowledge of the patient, however, because of the prevailing prejudice. In this respect the following fragment should prove interesting. This anecdote was related by Rudyard Kipling to a select company of doctors, members of the Royal Society of Medicine, at the Hotel Mayfair in London:

"Nearly three hundred years ago, Nicholas Culpeper, an astrologer-physician, was in practice in Spitalfields, and it happened that a friend's maid-servant fell sick, which the local practitioner diagnosed as plague. Culpeper was called in as a second opinion. When he arrived the family were packing up the beds, preparatory to going away and leaving the girl to die. He took charge. There was no silly nonsense about taking or looking for the characteristic plague tongue. He only asked at what hour the young woman had taken to her bed. He then erected a horoscope, and inquired of the face of the heavens how the malady might prove. The face of the heavens indicated that it was not plague, but just smallpox, which our ancestors treated as lightly as we do. And smallpox it turned out to be. So the family came back with their bedding and lived happily ever after, the girl recovered, and Culpeper said what he thought of his misguided fellow practitioner. Among other things he called him a man of forlorn fortunes with sore eyes."[3]

The arguments of astrology relative to religion, philosophy and science will be found under their proper headings in the various chapters of this book. From the data which we gathered it will be evident that in all ages philosophers and scientists of the greatest attainments have acknowledged that the motions and configurations of the heavenly bodies were the exciting causes of physical phenomena. In these pages will be found the astrologer as priest, the astrologer as prophet, the astrologer as king, the astrologer as statesman, the astrologer as scientist, the astrologer as philosopher and the astrologer as poet. Nor will the names be inconspicuous ones but rather the greatest of their several orders. No other science known to man can boast of such an illustrious following.

The case rests upon the facts.

[3] See *London Daily Express:* Nov. 16, 1928.

## THE ASTROLOGER'S PRAYER

"BUT lest my words be bereft of divine aid and the envy of some hateful man impugn them by hostile attacks, whoever thou art, God, who continuest day after day the course of the heavens in rapid rotation, who perpetuatest the mobile agitation of ocean's tides, who strengthenest earth's solidity in the immovable strength of its foundation, who refreshest with night's sleep the toil of our earthly bodies, who when our strength is renewed returnest the grace of sweetest light, who stirrest all the substance of thy work by the salutary breath of the winds, who pourest forth the waves of streams and fountains in tireless force, who revolvest the varied seasons by sure periods of days: sole Governor and Prince of all, sole Emperor and Lord, whom all the celestial forces serve, whose will is the substance of perfect work, by whose faultless laws all nature is forever adorned and regulated; thou Father alike and Mother of every thing, thou bound to thyself, Father and Son, by one bond of relationship; to Thee we extend suppliant hands, Thee with trembling supplication we venerate; grant us grace to attempt the explanation of the courses of thy stars; thine is the power that somehow impels us to that interpretation. With a mind pure and separated from all earthly thoughts and purged from every strain of sin we have written these books for thy Romans."

—FIRMICUS.

# THE STORY OF
# ASTROLOGY

*"Jacob's Staff Is Broken. The Brazen Astrolabe Is Green and Cankered. Dust and Cobwebs Cover the Tomes of Ptolemy and Haly: and the Garrets of Spitalfields and the Seven Dials Are Untenanted by the Seers, Who Whilome Dealt Out Their Awful Prognostications of Changes in Church and State, and Who Scowling Alike at Rome and at Constantinople, Ensured the Downfall of the Turk, and the Confusion of the Scarlet Harlot of the Seven Hills."* . . . QUARTERLY REVIEW.

## GENERAL SURVEY

ASTROLOGY is that ancient science which treats of the influence of the stars upon Nature and mankind. A horoscope is a map or diagram of the heavens cast for a particular moment of time, drawn on paper, and read according to well-established rules. The horoscope is calculated by a mathematical process, free from the elements of chance or divination. Predictions are deduced from the horoscope in a demonstrable and strict mathematical way, "according to a certain chain of causes which for ages past have been found uniformly to produce a correspondent train of effects."[1] The science of the stars, then, has not been established merely upon dogma and belief, but derives its authority from thousands of years of observation "by philosophers of the

[1] Raphael's *A Manual of Astrology.*

15

highest refinement." Astrology was practiced by the earliest civilized peoples of the earth, and in every period of philosophic and spiritual enlightenment was accorded a place of honor by those of high birth and great learning.

In his first book on *Divination,* Cicero observes that the Chaldeans had records of the stars for the space of 370,000 years; and Diodorus Siculus says that their observations comprehended the space of 473,000 years.[2] Cicero further maintains that the Babylonians over a period of many thousands of years kept the nativities (horoscopes) of all children who were born among them, and from this enormous mass of data calculated the effects of the various planets and zodiacal signs.

"The SUMERIANS and BABYLONIANS believed," writes Sir E. A. Wallis-Budge, "that the will of the gods in respect to man and his affairs could be learned by watching the motions of the stars and planets, and that skilled star-gazers could obtain from the motions and varying aspects of the heavenly bodies indications of future prosperity and calamity. They therefore caused observations to be made and recorded on tablets, which they interpreted from a magical and not astronomical point of view, and these observations and their comments on them, and interpretation of them, have formed the foundation of the astrology in use in the world for the last 5,000 years. According to ancient traditions preserved by Greek writers, the Babylonians made these observations for some hundreds of thousands of years, and though we must reject such fabulous statements, we are bound to believe that the period during which observa-

2 Thomas Taylor in *Notes on Julius Firmicus Maternus.* Epigenes, Berosus, and Critodemes set the duration of astronomical observations by the Babylonians at from 490,000 to 720,000 years. (Thorndike.)

tions of the heavens were made on the plains of Babylonia comprised many thousands of years."[3] What boasted science of the moderns can be said to be built upon a more substantial foundation?

Berosus, the initiated priest of Baal, was the first and greatest of the Chaldean astrologers and historiographers. He was a man of broad intellect and profound learning, and it is recorded of him that "nearly all his prophecies were fulfilled."[4] Berosus settled in the island state of Cos, and there established a school of the "secret sciences." He is described by Vitruvius as the forerunner of a long line of astrologers "of genius and great acuteness, who sprang directly from the nations of the Chaldeans."[5] The wisdom and skill of Berosus so deeply impressed the men of his age that it is reported of them that after his death they raised a statue to their priest and sage. As a testimony to the truth of the predictions made by Berosus, they caused this image to be cast with a golden tongue."[6]

The earliest Egyptian astrologers to be mentioned in manuscripts now known were the "godlike" Petosiris and Necepso. It is believed that the first of these "celebrated men," as Manetho calls them, was a king and the second a priest, and that they lived at approximately the time of Rameses II. Reference is made to these astromancers in the writings of Athereaus, Aristophanes, Juvenal, Pliny, Galen, Ptolemy and Suidas. From the testimony of these authors there can be little doubt that both Petosiris and Necepso left extensive writings on astrological subjects, but little has been preserved to

---

[3] See *Amulets and Superstitions.*
[4] Burgel's *Astronomy for All.*
[5] See *De Architectura.*
[6] Burgel's *Astronomy for All.*

this age. Even during the period of the later Greek writers these men were looked upon as semi-divine personages who had received their knowledge from Hermes and Asclepius. Several works now regarded as forgeries by conservative scholars were circulated under their names during the Gnostic period. If we review the astrology of Chaldea and Babylon, we are forced to agree with St. Justin that "from the first invention of the hieroglyphics it was not the vulgar, but the distinguished and select men who became initiated in the secrets of the temples into the science of every kind of astrology."

According to Albert Pike, the distinguished Masonic scholar, books on astrology were carried with the deepest reverence in the religious processionals of the Egyptians. The astrologers of Oxydraces came to Alexander the Great when he invaded India and explained to him certain of the secrets of the heavenly science. The Brahmans, whom Apollonius of Tyana visited in the first century of the Christian Era, were also deeply learned in the mysteries of the stars. In China, astrology set forth the rules by which both the state and the family were to be governed. The Arabians deemed it the mother of sciences. The astrologer Valens drew up by royal command the horoscope of Constantine the Great.[7]

After noting that the great Hermes, Ptolemy, King of Egypt, and Zoroaster, the first of the Magi, were patrons of astrology and had examined carefully into its mysteries, Her Royal Highness, Princess of Cumberland, wrote: "How ignorant and prejudiced, then, must that man be, and how crude with understanding, which condemns a science in which the wisest and greatest king of the earth, even Solomon, delighted." The original Ra-

[7] See *Morals and Dogma.*

phael (R. C. Smith), who styled himself, "the astrologer of the nineteenth century," declared that in former times astrology was comparable to a mighty colossus that overstrode all other sciences, and that even in this incredulous era it has "enlightened the gloomy atmosphere of unbelief" by some remarkable prediction. Astrology has well been denominated the "rule of kings," and by virtue of the excellence of the art itself has survived "the crash of empires, the vicissitudes of ages, and the revolutions of public opinion."[8]

The Egyptians maintained that the sciences of astrology and alchemy were bestowed upon man by the benevolence of the gods. The elder nations of the earth conceded the Egyptian premise, but each claimed that its own philosophers were the first to cultivate the "imperishable art." Astrology was practiced in India thousands of years before the compiling of the Vedas. The great magician and astrologer, Asuramaya, was born in Atlantis, thus testifying, upon the authority of the *Puranas*, to the extreme antiquity of the celestial science.[9] The oldest traditions of China are concerned, among other things, with the qualities and attributes of the five planetary emperors of the world and the dynasty of starry kings that preceded human rulers. Josephus, speakings for the Jews, affirms that Adam was instructed in astrology by heavenly inspiration. According to Diodorus, Hercules was accredited with having revealed the art to the Greeks, but this is probably an allegorical allusion to the sun. Lucian, however, held that Orpheus brought the principles of astrology from India, and that "the planets were signified by the seven strings of his lyre." Even in far-off Tibet astrology is practiced with

[8] Raphael's *A Manual of Astrology.*
[9] Blavatsky's *The Secret Doctrine.*

amazing accuracy by an involved system understood only by the Bon initiates. Prescott describes how the Aztec Indians, upon the birth of a child, instantly summoned an astrologer, whose duty was to ascertain the destiny of the new-born babe.[10] Indeed, there is no corner of the earth where those who are the wisest of their race and time have not read and pondered what James Gaffarel, astrologer to Cardinal Richelieu, so wisely termed "the handwriting on the wall of heaven."[11]

There have been many illustrious exponents of astrology, both ancient and modern; in fact few branches of learning have been more adequately represented or have won better patronage. Of the famous personages of the last few centuries addicted to the study of astrology, many must remain unknown; for, as Professor Max Mueller, the great Orientalist, has noted, while many of the greatest intellects have studied astrology, the majority have never expressed their opinions on the subject for fear of public criticism.

Among the poets whose verses defend the ancient art are such venerable names as Homer, Hesiod, Aratus, Aeschylus, Manilius, Horace, Virgil, Propertius, Macrobius, Juvenal, Chaucer, Dante, Milton, Dryden, Campbell, Byron, Scott (Sir Walter), Goethe, Schiller, and Shakespeare. In an article on astrology in the writings of Shakespeare, John Cook thus summarizes the results of an extensive research: "The numerous allusions to the practice of astrology, the striking metaphors, and apt illustrations, scattered throughout the plays of Shakespeare, at once attest his intimate acquaintance with the general principles of the science, and the popularity of astrological faith. . . . He has left us sufficient evidence

10 See *History of the Conquest of Mexico.*
11 See *Unheard of Curiosities*, etc.

to show that he was largely influenced by a subject which has left indelible marks in the language and literature of England." The bard of Avon puts the following words into the mouth of King Lear:

"It is the stars, the stars above us govern our conditions."

Even more striking is his flair for astrologic humor. He makes a disgruntled player to complain: "It is impossible that anything should be as I would have it; for I was born, Sir, when the Crab was ascending; and all my affairs go backwards."

Dante's astrology is written in majestic measure. We follow him into the vastness of space:

"........... I saw
The sign that follows Taurus, and was in it.
Oh glorious stars! Oh light impregnated
With mighty virtues, from which I acknowledge
All of my genius whatsoe'er it be,
With you was born, and hid himself with you
He who is father of all mortal life,
When first I tasted of the Tuscan air;
And then when grace was freely given to me
To enter the high wheel which turns you round
Your region was allotted unto me."[12]

"For Dante astrology was the noblest of the sciences," writes H. Flanders Dunbar, "For Dante," she continues, "the principle of individualization is the influence of planets and stars, or, more accurately, of the intelligences by which they are moved. The ego, created directly by God, in its connection with the body comes under stellar influence, and at birth is stamped like wax by a seal. All impressions from the stars are good, since there is no lovableness that does not reflect the lovable-

[12] *Paradiso*, Canto XXII. See Hungad's *A Brief History of Astrology.*

ness of God. It is the harmonizing and proportioning of
these good qualities in their true relationships that make
this or that person more or less perfect. It is likely that
the modern reader, with his oversimple conception of
astrology, will lose much of the meaning of Dante. . . .
Astrology was both more complicated and more scientific in method than the familiar birth-month pamphlets
suggest."[13]

Goethe commits himself in no uncertain terms to
both the theory and practice of astrology. He begins his
autobiography thus: "On the 28th of August 1749, at
mid-day, as the clock struck twelve, I came into the
world, at Frankfort-on-the-Maine. The aspect of the
stars was propitious: the sun stood in the sign of the Virgin, and had culminated for the day; Jupiter and Venus
looked on with a friendly eye, and Mercury not adversely; the attitude of Saturn and Mars was neutral;
the moon alone, just full, exerted all the more as she her
power of opposition had just reached her planetary
hour. She, therefore, resisted my birth which could not
be accomplished until this hour was passed. These auspicious aspects which the astrologers subsequently interpreted very favorably for me may have been the
causes of my preservation."

"Do not Christians and Heathens, Jews and Gentiles,
poets and philosophers," writes Sir Walter Scott, "unite
in allowing the starry influences?"

Nor is science represented by less impressive names.
According to Thorndike, "A trio of great names, Pliny,
Galen, and Ptolemy stand out above all others in the
history of science in the Roman Empire."[14] Needless to
say, all these distinguished thinkers not only admitted

[13] See *Symbolism in Medieval Thought.*
[14] See *History of Magic and Experimental Science.*

the influence of the planets upon human life but wrote at some length on the science of astrology. The names of other astrologer-scientists are certainly no less renowned; Hippocrates, the father of medicine; Vitruvius, the master of architecture; Placidus, the mathematician; Giordano Bruno, the martyr; Jerome Cardan, the mathematician; Copernicus,[15] Galileo,[16] Gassendi, Tycho Brahe, Regiomontanus, Kepler, Huygens and C. Flammarion,[17] the astronomers; Roger Bacon, the Benedictine monk; Sir Francis Bacon, the father of modern science; Baron Napier, of Merchistoun, the inventor of logarithms; Flamsteed, the first astronomer royal and founder of Greenwich Observatory; Sir Elias Ashmole, the founder of the Ashmolean Museum at Oxford; and Sir Christopher Heydon, who wrote a lengthy treatise in defense of judicial astrology.

Hippocrates predicted a great plague at Athens, which came to pass. An old woman, ignorant of the difference between astronomy and astrology, came to Greenwich Observatory to recover a bundle of linen she had lost. Flamsteed set up a horary chart and the linen was found in the place indicated by him. "In the traditions of astrology," wrote Sir Francis Bacon, "the natures and dispositions of men are not without truth distinguished from the predominances of the planets." Tycho Brahe declares, "The stars rule the lot of man." From the period of the early Romans "even to Kepler, who died

[15] See *Astronomy* by David Todd, Director Emeritus Amhurst College Observatory.

[16] See *Galileo* by Emile Namer. "Galileo himself father of modern science read his children's horoscopes, at their birth."

[17] Sepharial writes: "It will not surprise my readers to know that Flammarion, had a sincere belief in the influence of the stars in human life, and I remember to have read a very striking preface by him in a book by Ely Star, when I was reading up this subject in India." (Hungad)

in 1630," wrote Wm. Wynn Westcott, "it may be said that every astronomer was also an astrologer to some extent." Elias Ashmole used to speak at the annual astrologers' feast. Although Sir Isaac Newton is not generally considered a defender of astrology, he was led to the study of astronomy by the interest aroused through the reading of astrological books. It is recorded that when the astronomer Halley, of comet fame, made a slighting remark as to the value of astrology, Newton gently rebuked him thus: "I have studied the subject, Mr. Halley; you have not."

At this point it may be appropriate to insert three well authenticated accounts of astrological prediction. The high integrity of the authorities involved demands a respectful consideration of their statements. The Archbishop of St. Andrews, having a disease which baffled the physicians of England, sent to the Continent in 1552, begging assistance of the mathematician-astrologer, Jerome Cardan. After erecting the horoscope of the prelate by which the disease was discovered and cured, Cardan took his leave in these words: "I have been able to cure you of your sickness, but cannot change your destiny, nor prevent you from being hung." Eighteen years later this churchman was hung by order of the commissioners appointed by Mary, Queen Regent of Scotland.[18] As he was passing through the city of London on his return home, Cardan was also engaged to calculate the nativity of King Edward the Sixth.

The second relates to a celebrated prophecy by the noted astronomer, Tycho Brahe. From a study of the great comet of 1577, Brahe was led to declare that "in the north, in Finland, there should be born a prince who should lay waste Germany and vanish in 1632."

[18] See Lavrey's *History of England*.

Time proved the accuracy of the comet's warning. The prince, Gustavus Adolphus, was born in Finland, ravaged Germany during the Thirty Years' War, and died as the astronomer had predicted in 1632. The *Encyclopædia Britannica* comments thus upon the circumstance: "The fulfillment of the details of this prophecy suggests that Tycho Brahe had some basis of reason for his prediction." (!)

The third account is taken from Lord Bacon's *Essay on Prophecy*. His lordship writes: "When I was in France, I heard from one Doctor Pena, that the Queen Mother, who was given to curious arts, caused the king her husband's nativity to be calculated, under a false name; and the astrologer gave a judgment, that he would be killed in a duell; at which the Queen laughed, thinking her husband to be above challenges and duells; but was slain, upon a course at tilt, the splinters of the staffe of Montgomery going in at his bever."

A goodly number of theologians have not found astrology incompatible with their religious tenets. It is scarcely necessary to advance evidence of the presence of astrological dogma in the sacred writings of the pagan and Christian worlds. The scriptures of the Brahmans, Taoists, Lamas, and other Oriental sects are replete with allusions to the influence of the heavenly bodies; and from the stars that fought against Sisera to the morning star of *Revelation*, the Bible of the Jews and Christians lends its testimony to the validity of astrology and astromancy. A few names come to mind, not to mention the semi-divine prophets and World Saviors. What Alphonso the Great says of Jesus Christ is true also of these other Redeemers, namely, that their whole history is written in the stars. The list includes Origen, the Ante-Nicean Father, and Bede, surnamed the Venerable. St. Augustine admitted the accuracy of astrology, but attributed the science to infernal agencies. Albertus Magnus, beatified bishop and architect, and his disciple, the great St. Thomas Aquinas (the latter one of the most learned of medieval divines), both acknowledged the power of the planets over mundane affairs. "All that Nature and art produces," wrote Albertus Magnus, "is driven by celestial powers." And St. Thomas Aquinas adds: "The celestial bodies are the cause of all that takes place in this sublunar world." Then there was Maimonides, Philip Melanchthon, the Rev. Dr. Butler, "Protestant Minister of the True, Ancient, Catholick, and Apostolik Faith of the Church of England," and Jacob Boehme, the seer of Seidenburg, not to mention His Eminence, the Cardinal, Duc de Richelieu, and the great Jesuit scholar, Athanasius Kircher.

The Holy See can boast of several astrologer-Popes: Sylvester (992–1002 A.D.), John XX,, John XXI, Sixtus IV, Julius II, Alexander IV, Leo X, Paul III, Clement VII and Calixtus III. According to Temple Hungad, Marsilio Ficino, the astrologer to the household of Lorenzo the Magnificent, casting the horoscopes of the children of that illustrious de Medici, predicted that little Giovanni was destined to become a Pope. When, later, this occurred and he ascended to the holy chair as Pope Leo X, he became a distinguished patron of astrology and a great believer in the ancient science. Pope Julius II had the day of his coronation set by astrology; Sixtus IV arranged his audiences according to planetary hours; and it is said of Paul III that he never held a consistory except when the heavenly bodies were propitious.[19]

So numerous are the rulers, statesmen, and warriors

19 See Hungad's *A Brief History of Astrology*.

who have believed in astrology and mapped their earthly courses from the stars, that only a few outstanding examples can be cited here. The four greatest conquerors of historic times—Alexander of Macedon, Julius Caesar, Genghis Khan, and Napoleon I—devoutly believed in the "heavenly" government of the world. The Brahman sages revealed to Alexander not only the time of his death but the manner thereof—that he should perish from a cup. When Alexander reached the walls of Babylon the astrologers warned him away, saying, "Flee from this town where thy fatal star reigns." Alexander was deeply impressed by this warning and for a time turned aside from Babylon. But later he entered the city where he came by his death. According to Lucian, Caesar noted the revolutions of the stars in the midst of his preparations for battle. The mathematician, Spurina, warned the immortal Julius that his Mars threatened violence during the Ides of March. Genghis Khan appointed astrologers to positions of honor in his suite, and one of them, Ye Liu Chutsai, a Chinese, was his constant adviser during the Kha Khan's victorious march across half the world. Napoleon pointed out his guiding star to Cardinal Fesch, his uncle, but that worthy churchman had not the vision to perceive it. The first Emperor of the French put such faith in the "testimony of the suns" that he frequently sought the advice of the celebrated French seeress, Mlle. Lenormand. In justice to the ability of this remarkable woman, it should be remembered that she warned him repeatedly against a Russian campaign. Napoleon's fall was largely due to a futile attempt to outwit his Saturn, which raised him up only to cast him down. "Wallenstein in his tower consulting the portents of fate; Josephine, extending her hand not yet imperial, to the sable fortune-teller; Napoleon, trusting to the star of his destiny, and following it from victory to victory and from triumph to triumph till it burst forth as 'the sun of Austerlitz'; these and examples like these, exercise a strange fascination over the feelings which is not wholly due to the magnitude of the interests or the eminence of the personages with which such fancies are entwined."[20]

Darius, Emperor of Persia, relied upon the words of his venerable astrologer, Al Hakim, which means "the wise one." Al Hakim wrote, among other books, one entitled *Judicia Gjmaspis,* wherein "he predicted that Jesus would appear; that Mohammed should be born; and that the Magian religion should be abolished, etc." Among the Arabs there arose illustrious scientist-astrologers, whose learning was frequently resorted to by the princes of the state. Such names as Alkindi, Albumasar, Thebit ben Corat, and Rhazes mean little to Western scholars. But by the Moslem these astrologers are regarded as men of extraordinary merit. The annals of the Ottoman Empire record that the rise of the Turk was due to the holy astrologer who predicted that Othman I "should be the brightest star of the East, and that his posterity should reign over seven climates." The successors of Othman continued their patronage of astrology even to the glorious Solyman II, under whose able leadership the Ottoman Empire reached the zenith of its power.

Medieval Europe derived its astrology from Arabia and the Roman Empire. The Moors of Spain cultivated the art, which became essentially a part of a scientific education. Astrology, according to Alphonso of Castile, surnamed "The Wise," is one of the liberal sciences, "and according to the law, the free practice thereof is

[20] G. F. H. in *The Southern Magazine.*

granted to such as be masters therein and understand it truly: For the judgments and predictions which are given by this art are discerned in the natural course of the planets, and are taken from the books of Ptolemy and the other wise masters, who have labored therein." The rise of the European states, which for centuries eyed each other with mutual suspicion, gave a tremendous impetus to judicial astrology. Astrology was accorded scholastic recognition in the Middle Ages. There were professors of the art in the great universities of Parma, Bologna and at the Sapienza.[21] The city of Florence maintained a city astrologer in much the same way that a modern community maintains a health officer.[22] Petty princes and feudal lords retained their Merlins. In this way astrology became a most potent force in national policy, even as at the present time it is more or less apparent in the operation of the stock exchange. Volumes would be required to even outline the history of astrology from the Dark Ages to the present. We will limit ourselves to a few examples picked more or less at random.

Sir Henry Cornelius Agrippa was astrologer to Charles the First of France, but lost that office because of the consistent manner in which he predicted misfortune. King Charles the Seventh of France is said to have attended classes in astrology. Catherine de Medici was profoundly versed in the heavenly lore and was the patroness of Nostradamus, the most famous of the French astrologers and physician to King Henry the Second and Charles the Ninth. The prophecies of Nostradamus, "set forth in a pamphlet, were read all over the world. Although he died in 1566, his forebodings were believed

[21] See *The Jewish Encyclopedia.*
[22] See *Religions Past and Present,* by Bertram C. A. Windle.

in as late as the eighteenth century, for at its beginning a Papal Edict forbade the sale of the booklet, as it proclaimed the downfall of the Papacy."[23] He also prophesied the great fire of London in 1666, the French Revolution, and the advent of Napoleon, centuries before these circumstances took place, and in the case of Napoleon gave a very accurate description of his person and temperament. Nostradamus' predictions of the London fire is as follows:

> "The blood o' th' just requires,
> Which out of London reeks,
> That it be raz'd with fires,
> In year threescore and six."

At the time when Queen Anne of Austria, the wife of Louis the Thirteenth, was delivered of the Dauphin, afterward Louis the Fourteenth, a famous German astrologer was in attendance to calculate the nativity of the young prince. After setting up the chart, the astrologer, however, refused to give over three words in his judgment thereof: "Diu, dure, féliciter."[24] Nothing more could have been said which would sum up more truthfully the reign of Louis the Fourteenth. After reaching more mature years, Louis the Fourteenth also dabbled in the astral science.

Louis XI consulted the astrologers Angelo Catto and d'Almonsor and maintained in royal style the celebrated astrologer Galeotti Martius. The latter is described by Sir Walter Scott in these glowing terms:

"Martius was none of those ascetic, withered, pale professors of mystic learning of those days, who bleared their eyes over the midnight furnace, and macerated

---

[23] Burgel's *Astronomy for All.*
[24] Limier's *Hist. du Règne de Louis XIV.*

their bodies by out-matching the polar bear. He was trained in arms and renowned as a wrestler. His apartment was splendidly furnished, and on a large oaken table lay a variety of mathematical and astrological instruments, all of the most rich materials and curious workmanship. His astrolabe of silver was the gift of the Emperor of Germany and his Jacob's staff of ebony jointed with gold, was a mark of esteem from the reigning Pope. In person, the astrologer was a tall, bulky, yet stately man. His features though rather overgrown were dignified and noble, and a Samson might have envied the dark downward sweep of his long descending beard. His dress was a chamber-robe of the richest Genoa velvet, with ample sleeves clasped with frogs of gold and lined with sables. It was fastened round his middle by a broad belt of virgin parchment, round which were represented in crimson characters the signs of the Zodiac."[25]

Guido Bonatus, a famous Italian astrologer, was renowned for the uncanny accuracy of his predictions. Finding himself in a besieged Italian city, he conferred with the chief military official of that city, the Earl of Montserrat, as to the proper time to lead out his army against the besiegers. Bonatus finally decided upon the auspicious moment, declaring that the sally would be successful, but an unfortunate aspect showed that the Earl would receive a slight wound in the knee. So certain was the astrologer that when he accompanied the Earl on the sortie, he carried with him the necessary dressings. The prediction was fulfilled to the letter. The enemy was routed, but in the melee the Earl received a slight wound exactly as Bonatus had described, and up rushed the astrologer with lints and bandages. We have

[25] See Thompson's *The Mystery and Romance of Astrology.*

no record of Bonatus saying, "I told you so!" but it would have been an unequalled opportunity.

Astrologers were also important personages at the court of England; Charles the First, and Oliver Crom-

*Horoscope of Queen Elizabeth*—from Sibly's *Astrology.*

well turned to the stars in times of distress. Even Good Queen Bess, who stamped her foot at comets' tails, "adhered firmly to her belief in astrology." Lord Burleigh is supposed to have calculated the nativity of Elizabeth and the celebrated Dr. Dee of Mortlake "fixed the date of her coronation from figures drawn up at the request of Dudley."[26] Elizabeth so highly respected the scholarship of Dr. Dee that she made him Chancellor of St. Paul's.

The famous English astrologer, William Lilly, was called before the House of Commons, where he was informed that as he had fifteen years before predicted the plague and the great fire of London, they desired to know from him the causes or authors thereof. William Lilly replied that he had been able to discover no cause, therefore he must attribute the conflagration to the immediate finger of God. King Charles I consulted Lilly as to his fate and was advised to travel in an eastward direction for safety. Instead he journeyed westward, with the tragic results recorded in history. In recognition of his astrological ability, Lilly was presented with a gold chain and medal by Charles the Tenth of Sweden.

Astrology also played a part at the inception of the United States. A man who is known to have been proficient in astrology was present in an advisory capacity at meetings attended by George Washington and Benjamin Franklin.[27] There is also a persistent rumor that Thomas Jefferson collected the horoscopes of famous persons.

Philosophers, historians, and mystics not only admit the reasonableness of astrology, but not a few of them were proficient in the art. All the following have either convinced themselves that astrology was true or else have sympathetically recorded the learning of older masters. The list is impressive and includes Thales, Anaxagoras, Anaximander, Herodotus, Pythagoras, Heraclitus, Plato, Aristotle, Eudoxus, Seneca, Cicero, Josephus, Philo Ju-

[26] See *Macmillan's Magazine.*
[27] See Campbell's *Our Flag.*

daicus, Eusebius, Diodorus, Varro, Porphyry, Plotinus, Proclus, Iamblichus, Heracleides, Ponticus, Tacitus, Apuleius, Phornutus, Apollonius of Tyana, Paracelsus, Bulwer-Lytton, Spinoza, Leibnitz, St.-Germain, Cagliostro, Eliphas Levi, and Blavatsky. Even Descartes was forced to grudgingly admit the accuracy of an astrological prediction. Thales predicted an eclipse, the darkness of which stopped a battle between the Medes and the Lydians, and to prove that philosophers can be wealthy, cast a horoscope of the olive crop, and by buying up the presses quickly amassed a fortune. Referring to the matter of prophecy, Cicero wrote: "The existence of the powers of divination must be conceded . . . We see it, and hear it, and read of it, and have inherited it from our forefathers." H. P. Blavatsky writes: "Astrology is a science *as infallible* as astronomy itself, with the condition, however, that its interpreters must be equally infallible . . . Astrology is to exact astronomy what psychology is to exact physiology."[28] Richard A. Proctor also observes: "None of the races of antiquity rose *above* a certain level of civilization without developing a belief in the influence of the heavenly bodies, and without devising systems for reading and ruling the planets."[29]

Of astrology, as of the oracle at Delphi, it may be said that it "revealed many a tyrant and foretold his fate. Through its means many an unhappy being was saved from destruction and many a perplexed mortal guided in the right way. It encouraged useful institutions, and promoted the progress of useful discoveries. Its moral influence was on the side of virtue, and its political influence in favor of the advancement of civil liberty."[30]

[28] See *Isis Unveiled.*
[29] See *Old and New Astronomy.*
[30] Gardner's *Faiths of the World.*

Tortured as a sorcerer in one era, ridiculed as a charlatan in another, and raised to highest honors in more generous times, the astrologer has survived the numerous "physical changes in the moral and intellectual world." Like the fabled phoenix of old, astrology has risen again and again victoriously from its own ashes. Vilified and traduced by the sophists of every age, but vindicated and evidenced by Nature herself, astrology still gathers lustre from its own stars, and now in the twentieth century it may truthfully be said that the whole civilized world is astrology conscious.

# THE ASTROLOGY OF THE CHINESE
## AND TIBETANS

*"The Annals of China, a Country Never Backward in Claiming the Invention of Almost Everything, New or Old, on the Earth or in the Sky, Ascribe the Formation of Constellations to Tajao, the Prime Minister of Hwang Ti, 2637 B. C., and Make Much of an Observation of the Pleiades, 2537 B. C., from an Observatory Said to Have Been Erected 2608 B. C. But Real Stellar Work in That Country Seems to Have Begun Only About Ten or Twelve Centuries Before Our Era, and Then Almost Solely in the Interest of Astrology."*—RICHARD H. ALLEN.

MODERN astronomers are reticent to admit that they are the step-sons of an occult science. Yet "we would not possess astronomy today," according to Paul Carus, "had not our ancestors been given to astrology."[1] Costard regretfully concurs in the admission. "Astronomy, I am afraid," he says, "originally owes its birth and progress to astrology."[2] The isolated position occupied by China and its almost complete freedom from foreign influence for several thousand years rendered it necessary for the Chinese to discover, develop, and perfect their arts and sciences without benefit of the accumulated knowledge of other races. To the Chinese, the outside world did not exist, and beyond the gates of China was nothing but abyssmal space.

This national psychology is a vital factor in a critical analysis of Chinese thought and gravitates decidedly against the popular belief that the Chinese derived their astrology from the Arabs or the Hindus. We trust that

[1] See *Chinese Thought.*
[2] See *History of Astronomy.*

this time-honored controversy has finally been settled for Occidental scholars by the recent decision of T. E. R. Phillips, the Honorable Secretary of the Royal Astronomical Society. This gentleman writes: "The ancient Chinese zodiac is quite independent of that in use in the west." And further on he adds: "It is clear that China was one of the leading nations of antiquity in astronomical study."[3]

The ancient empire, then, supplies a complete and uninfluenced example of material sciences inevitably developing from occult or metaphysical origins. It is true that modern Chinese astrology has been profoundly influenced by recent contact with European civilization, but it is also true that the latter culture is utterly distinct from the older learning. The modifications of early systems and the new interpretations given to ancient doctrines, which resulted from the introduction of Jesuitism in Cathay, should not deceive the critical investigator nor lead him to depreciate the profound significance of the indigenous arts, traditions, and sciences. Gaubil summarizes the opinions of Jesuit scholars to the effect that the Chinese presumed the relationships existing between terrestrial rulers and their subjects to be controlled by the motions and positions of celestial bodies and other sidereal phenomena; and it was to discover these relationships that the Chinese astronomers of all ages primarily directed their efforts.[4]

We are indebted to A. J. Pearce for the following excellent historical summary. "Astrology," he says, "was firmly established among the learned Chinese from the earliest periods in the history of their remarkable country. From the days of Fohi, about 2752 years B. C., for

[3] See *Splendour of the Heavens.*
[4] See *History of Chinese Astronomy.*

nearly 2500 years, Sir David Brewster said, astronomy was studied in China solely for the purposes of astrology; and it was held in the highest veneration—Emperors being chosen on account of their knowledge of astronomy and astrology. This was expressly the case with Chueni, in the year 2513 B. C., who himself computed an ephemeris of the motions of the five planets, a great conjunction of which is thought to have been observed by him, as it took place in the year 2449 B. C."[5] Even Ser Marco Polo makes mention of the Oriental astrologers and the esteem which was accorded them. "These astrologers," writes the great traveler, "are very skillful in their business, and often their words come to pass, so the people have great faith in them."[6]

Fohi, the Divine Emperor, who is variously referred to as the Dragon Man, the Supreme Emperor, the Sage, and the Father of gods and men, was an avatara of the eternal divinity, *Luminous Heaven.* It is written of Fohi that he was born of a virgin "without the concurrence of a father." Fohi had the head of a man and the body of a serpent and, like the Chaldean Oannes, was the first educator of the Chinese. "He taught them to use written characters, for which he is designated 'the literary ancestor of the myriad of ages;' he invented the Diagrams to teach men the formation of the universe from chaos, the succession of worlds, etc.; he instituted marriage; instructed mankind in hunting and fishing and all useful arts; and reared 'the six kinds of animals,' some for food and some for sacrificing to the Gods. He was himself the first sacrificer, and his name signifies 'the Victim.' "[7] Fohi, as the Son of Heaven, was informed in all the mys-

[5] See *The Horoscope,* Vol. I.
[6] See *The Book of Ser Marco Polo.*
[7] See Appendix to McClatchie's Translation of *The Yih King.*

teries of the firmament and, among other boons, bestowed upon mankind the knowledge of divination by elements, planets, and curious arbitrary symbols. It is written in the *Shu King*, "Of the Five Disposers, the first is called the year; the second is called the Moon; the third is named the Sun; the fourth is the planetary hour; and the fifth is known as the astronomical dispositions."

Confucius is unquestionably the outstanding ethical force in China. Although he admitted his inability to comprehend the metaphysical abstractions of Lao-tse, he was nevertheless a man of profound mentality, with a firm grasp upon the practical issues of life. His birth was announced by a strange vision in which five ancient and mysterious sages appeared leading in their midst a lion-like creature covered with the scales of a dragon and carrying a short horn in the middle of its forehead. This annunciation is susceptible of an astrological rendering. The dragon-lion of China, like the phoenix of Arabia and Egypt, signifies a certain time cycle, and at the climax of each such cycle the heavens produces a "superior man." The five ancient sages, like the five sidereal emperors, were the planets, which added further testimony to that of the cycle; for they are spoken of as bringing in or leading the sacred animal.

The attitude of Confucius towards matters of divination in general and of the heavenly mysteries in particular may be inferred from his devotion to *The Yih King*, the earliest known magical and metaphysical writing of the Chinese, for which he prepared an elaborate commentary. Of this classic, one writer has said: "The Yih King is one of the most ancient, most curious, and most mysterious documents in the world. It is more mysterious than the Pyramids of Egypt, more ancient than the Vedas of India, more curious than the cuneiform in-

scriptions of Babylon."[8] That Confucius believed in predestination and the inevitability of cycles is evident from
the strange circumstance preceding his death. The sacred
animal by which his birth was announced was killed one
day in the forest, and the sage realized this to foretell
the end of the cycle of his ministry. Being, therefore,
already in great age, he prepared for death. A few sen-
tences from the writings of Confucius suggest his familiarity with astrological principles. "In order to know
men, he may not dispense with a knowledge of heaven."
Again: "Without recognizing the ordinances of heaven,
it is impossible to be a superior man." Or again: "Good
and evil do not wrongly befall men, but heaven sends
down misery or happiness according to their conduct."
And lastly: "Calamities sent by heaven may be avoided,
but from calamities brought on by one's self there is no
escape."[9]

A curious episode in Chinese history is reminiscent
of the burning of the Alexandrian library. When the
She Hwang-ti became Emperor of all China, he ordered
the burning of the ancient books and the destruction of
all the fragments of primordial learning. It is generally
supposed that he did this through a dislike for books
due to personal illiteracy, but an examination of the
facts reveals this to have been impossible. The libraries
were destroyed because the Emperor believed that the
promiscuous reading of the ancient classics would result
in the misinterpretation of profound issues and thereby
endanger the integrity of the state. According to Li-sze,
the "ancient works ought only to be in the library of the
Emperor." According to present records, books on astrology were excepted from the edict of destruction, pos-

8 Carus's *Chinese Thought.*
9 Dawson's *The Ethics of Confucius.*

sibly because it was realized that this learning was essential to the administration of the state and was of a heavenly rather than mortal origin.[10]

The astrolatry of the Chinese is established upon the line of imperial descent, for under the old regime the Emperor was the Son of Heaven, the direct descendant of the azure God of the Sky. Among the most important ceremonials of the empire was the annual celebration of the happy new year, which took place on the night of the winter solstice when Yang, the Spirit of Light, began to increase. To the south of the great city of Peking stands the altar of heaven in the midst of an imaginary wheel made up of the philosophic diagrams of Fohi. The altar is circular in shape and rises in three tiers, each level being surrounded by a carved marble balustrade. Upon the night of the winter solstice the whole area in which the altar stands was weirdly lighted by torches. On the upper terrace, or altar proper, there stood a tablet bearing the inscription, "Imperial Heaven, Supreme Emperor." There were also rows of similar tablets dedicated to emperors of the divine line who have intervened between the first divine emperor and his then worshipping descendant. Upon the second terrace were tablets to the sun, the moon, the five planets, the Great Bear, the 28 principal constellations (lunar mansions), and the other important stars of heaven. The princes of the realm, the great mandarins, and other dignitaries all stood in their appointed places during the ceremony. When everything was in readiness, the Emperor ascended into the presence of the tablet of "High Heaven" and bowing humbly before the venerable past, knelt and knocked his forehead against the marble pavement, beseeching the Great Emperor above to

[10] Fergusson's *Chinese Researches.*

look with favor upon his earthly son and to protect the empire.

The Chicago Daily News once published an article on astrology, attributed to the London Daily Mail. It states that "the Emperor of China is a true believer in Astrology, and he has ordered his official Astrologers to search for a propitious day for the return of the court to Pekin."[11]

Of Tibetan astrology we will only note that it was first disseminated by the illustrious Padma Sambhava, the Lotus-Born, more often referred to as "The Precious Guru," who traveled from India, where he was a professor in the great Buddhist University of Nalanda, to Tibet. In that country he founded Lamaism about the year 749 A.D.[12] From the time of the Precious Guru to the present, astrology has been constantly employed by the Tibetans in determining not only every action of life but also the conditions of the soul in the after-death state. "The Buddhists are all believers in planetary influence," writes Pearce, "their very religion being founded upon this belief. For 5,000 years, at least, this belief has been accepted by hundreds of millions of Buddhists, Chinese, Hindus, etc. No mere delusion could have swayed the minds of learned Buddhists for so many thousand of years."[13] As in that part of Tibet contiguous to China, Tibetan astrology takes on a Chinese aspect, so in those parts lying close to India, it shows a marked Indian influence. Tibetan astrologers do not make use of an ephemeris, their calculations being from fixed cycles rather than from actual planetary positions. Strangely, enough, their system is amazingly accurate,

11 See *Star of the Magi*, June, 1901.
12 See Evans-Wentz's *The Tibetan Book of the Dead*.
13 See *The Horoscope*, Vol. I.

and their method—the secret of which they zealously guard—compares favorably in the matter of results with the more complicated Brahmanic and Ptolemaic schools. A brief account of Tibetan astrology will be found in Waddell's *Buddhism of Tibet.*

# THE ASTROLOGY OF THE HINDUS

*"To the Religious Hindu and to All Men of Moral Aspirations
a Knowledge of Astrology is Simply Invaluable and Indispensable.
His Aims Are Higher and All His Acts Are Regulated with Refer-
ence to the Existence of Nobler Lives in Future States of Existence.
A Knowledge of the Future Can Never Be Despised and Remedies
Taken to Improve Our Present Condition in the Light of Such
Knowledge Will Be Highly Useful in Our Practical Life."*—B.
SURYANARAIN ROW, M.R.A.S.

IT may be appropriate to open our brief consideration
of Hindu astrology with the invocation of Varaha Mi-
hira as it appears in the opening *sloka* of the *Brihat
Jataka*: "May the Sun, who gives form to the Moon,
who is the soul of the sages, who is the object of worship
among those who perform sacrifices, who is the chief
among the gods, planets and stars, who is the author for
destruction, creation and preservation of all the worlds,
who is invoked in the Vedas in various ways,—may that
Sun of variegated rays, the light of the three worlds,
give us speech."

An examination of the Vedas, Puranas, and other re-
ligio-historical documents of the ancient Aryans seems
to fully justify the claim for the priority of Hindu astrology as advanced by V. Subrahmanya Sastri. In the
preface to his translation of the *Brihat Jataka*, Mr. Sastri makes the unqualified statement that "the Hindus
are the oldest surviving nation in the world and astrology is their oldest science." Sir William Jones, the distinguished Orientalist, defends the antiquity of the
Hindu zodiac against the prevailing opinions of West-

44

ern scholars that it had been derived late from the learning of foreign nations. "In the first place," Jones declares, "the Brahmins were always too proud to borrow their science from the Greeks, Arabs, Moghuls or any nation of Mlechchhas, as they call those who are ignorant of the Vedas and have not studied the language of the Gods."[1] This opinion is also held by Walter Old (Sepharial), who declares that the conclusions of the so-called authorities who disparage the antiquity of Hindu astrology are disqualified on the grounds that "not one of them has familiarity with the subject of astrology, either European or Hindu."[2]

Dr. V. G. Rele is also convinced that the astrology of the Hindu is indigenous. "That the antiquity of the Indian Astrology," he notes, "is as remote as the Vedas, is a fact which is not difficult to prove. It forms one of the Angas of the Atharva-Veda." After observing that the *Jyotish Shastra;* a work devoted to the movements of the celestial bodies and their significance, is mentioned in the *Atharva-Veda,* he concludes: "It will thus be seen that the origin of the present Astrology is to be found in the Atharva-Veda-Jyotish the probable date of which, according to Dixit, and others is 900 to 1500 B. C."[3]

From the mass of evidence, of which the above is only representative, it seems reasonable to infer that India was indebted to neither the Greek nor the Moslem for its astrological doctrines, but rather to its own sages who lived in prehistoric times for its learning and proficiency in the various departments of genethlialogy. It is not impossible—in fact, there is considerable supporting evidence in the literary fragments of the classical pagans—

[1] See *Asiatic Researches.*
[2] See *The Science of Foreknowledge.*
[3] See *An Exposition of the Directional Astrology of the Hindus,* etc.

that the entire structure of Chaldean, Egyptian, Greek, and Roman learning, especially the more occult sciences, was originally derived from Asia. It is recorded of both the Egyptian Osiris and the Greek Orpheus that they were "dark skinned men" from the East, who brought the first knowledge of the sacred sciences from a race or order of sages who passed an almost fabled existence amidst the highlands of northern Hindustan. In fact, it has even been advanced that the modern Hindus received their spiritual traditions from an older race of Arhats. The Chinese have a similar record as to the source of their metaphysical culture, for reference is made in the sacred literature of the Tian-Ta'i sect to "The Great Teachers of the Snowy Mountains, the school of the Haimavatas," and also to "The great professors of the highest order who live in mountain depths remote from men."[4]

We must recognize Hindu astrology to be established upon the highest spiritual authority. The sciences of the Brahmins were founded by a line of antediluvian patriarchs who, perfected in all human virtues, communed with the Gods. Such sages were termed *Rishis*, a word which, according to Colebrooke, means an inspired writer or a saint through whom a deity reveals some knowledge to mankind. The Maharishis were the greatest of the sages and correspond somewhat with such prophets of the ancient Jews as Noah, Abraham, Jacob, and Moses. "Astrological works were originally composed by the great Maharishis Vasista, Parasara, Vyasa, Gargi, Marichi, Attri, Surya, Pitmaha, Bharadwaja, and Jaimini. They were persons endowed with the *Divya Drishti* (superior sight).[5] Parasara, whose works on as-

---

[4] See Beal's *Catena of Buddhist Scriptures,* etc.
[5] See *Introduction to Jataka Chundrika.*

trology are especially esteemed, was the father of Vyasa, who compiled the Vedas and Puranas, and whose name is venerated above that of almost any other mortal throughout the length and breadth of Hindustan.

There is an old Hindu legend which brings out a very subtle phase of astrological philosophy. The story is in substance as follows: Vishnu, the second person of the Hindu triad, while reposing calmly on his heavenly throne, thought of casting a look at his own nativity, and found in it that the next nineteen years of his life were under the malefic influence of Saturn; so, in order if possible to evade it, and to defeat Saturn, Vishnu transformed himself into the shape of an elephant, and spent the nineteen years in a dense forest, eating grass and other vegetables, fearing lest Saturn would inflict on him insufferable punishment had he remained in his divine shape. When the nineteen years had elapsed, Vishnu resumed his real form and throne, and while sitting there he one day saw Saturn passing by, and calling to him, asked: "How was it, Saturn, that you were not able to do me any injury in the nineteen years in which you had power over me?" "Why, sir," replied Saturn, "what can we poor subordinates do to such exalted gods as you are, except that for nineteen years you have been eating nothing but grass, and passing a most miserable life indeed, tormented by flies and mosquitoes."[6]

An example of Indian astrolatry may not be amiss at this point. Both Max Mueller and Sir William Jones have noted that the word *Rishi* is derived from a root which means "to shine." The word *Risksha*, now interpreted "shiner," means also a constellation and, strangely enough, a bear:[7] As *Maha* signifies "great," Maharishi

6 See *Star of the Magi*, Feb., 1902.
7 See Max Mueller's *Lectures on Language, Second Series*, viii.

| SUKRA (Venus) | RAVI (Sun) | BUDA (Mercury) | KETU (Dragon's Tail) |
|---|---|---|---|
| | HOROSCOPE *of* RAMA | | LAGNA CHUNDRA (Moon) GURU (Jupiter) |
| KUJA (Mars) | | | |
| RAHU (Dragon's Head) | | SANI (Saturn) | |

*Horoscope of Rama*—From the *Jataka Chundrika*.

may be interpreted "the great shiner"; Maharishis, the Great Constellation, or the Great Bear. This probably accounts for the present belief that the Seven Rishis have taken up their abode in the seven stars of the Constellation of Ursa Major which, in Hindu astronomy, bear their names.[8] Ancient navigators steered their courses from the Pole Star, which they discovered from the Great Dipper. The Rishis, then, point out the way —the Bear guards the Pole. The seven Rishis dwell together in the Polar Shamballah—the City of the Gods. In Hindu astrology "the Seven Suns of the Dragon of Wisdom" control the destiny of the world.

[8] See Brennand's *Hindu Astronomy*.

Brennand also calls attention to another interesting feature of Hindu astrosophy. In addition to the solar zodiac, there was a division of the ecliptic into twenty-eight parts, which corresponded with a similar number of constellations deriving their boundaries from the daily progress of the moon, and were called the lunar mansions. "It would appear," writes this author, "that the Solar Zodiac was made the principal foundation of the Western Astronomies of Egypt and Greece, and, in connection with its symbols, their respective systems of Mythology were formed; but in the more Eastern countries (especially in India), in the earliest ages, although the Solar Zodiac was retained, a preference would seem to have been given to the Lunar mansions, from which were constructed the Lunar and Luni-Solar Years.[9] Through this symbolism, in which the sun and the moon vied with each other, a division was effected in human society. Two ancient races of Indian princes, descendants of Manu, perpetuated the astronomical schism, being called "the Children of the Sun, and the Children of the Moon." They are the Suryas and the Chandravansas, pertaining to the solar and lunar dynasties respectively. So long as Western scholars remain ignorant of the less evident interpretations of these mysteries, they can scarcely hope to interpret either the science or metaphysics of Asia.

The *Ramayana* of Valmiki is a great epic poem, by some regarded as the original of the *Iliad*. It deals with the life of Rama, an avatara of Vishnu. Rama's beloved wife, Sita, had been abducted by Ravana, the wicked king of Lanka, or Ceylon. Gathering an army of monkeys, birds, and other creatures, Rama, aided by the ape-king, Hanuman, overcame Ravana together with his legions

[9] See Brennand's *Hindu Astronomy.*

of evil *rakshasas*, and rescued Sita. The horoscope of
Rama is an exceedingly fitting example of Hindu astrology and is preserved by Valmiki in the eighteenth chap-
ter of the *Bala Kanda*. The data is given as follows:
"Rama was born in Kataka with Chundra and Guru
there, Sani in Thula, Kuja in Makara, Sukra in Meena,
Ravi in Mesha and Buda in Vrishabha."[10] Translated
into English, this means that Cancer was rising, with
the moon in conjunction with Jupiter in the same sign.
Saturn was in Libra, Mars in Capricorn, Venus in Pisces,
the sun in Aries, and Mercury in Taurus. The Dragon's
Head is calculated in Sagittarius. According to Sepharial, it is probable that the horoscope is of a man born
prior to 3102 B.C., and under such conditions would
be one of the earliest horoscopes available for public
examination.[11]

In passing, it should be noted that Hindu astrology
differs from that of Ptolemy in one very definite particular. The Oriental calculations are based upon what
has been termed a natural zodiac, while that of Occidental peoples is based upon what is called an intellectual zodiac. Approximately 1400 years have passed
since these two zodiacs coincided, and there is now a
discrepancy of some 20 degrees between the two systems. The Oriental zodiac is, therefore, about 20 degrees
behind the Ptolemaic, and in applying Hindu keywords
to horoscopes set up according to the Western methods,
this difference must be taken into consideration.

10 See *Jataka Chundrika*.
11 See *The Science of Foreknowledge*.

# THE ASTROLOGY OF THE GREEKS

*"The Earliest Reference to Astrology Among the Greeks Appears to Be Plato,* TIM. 40 C 9. . . . *That Is Quite General, But Theophrastus Was More Definite.* . . . *The Stoics and Especially Poseidonios, Were Responsible for the Introduction of Astrology Into Greece."*—JOHN BURNET.

NECTANEBUS, the magician, according to Budge, was the last of the native kings of ancient Egypt. He was learned in all the transcendental arts and devoted to astrology. His occult knowledge enabled Nectanebus to circumvent the numerous conspirators who plotted his destruction. He also fashioned figurines of wax and clay, arraying them upon a huge table in the form of armies drawn up for battle. By enchantments and spells he then caused the figures representing his own soldiery to be victorious over another group which he had designated the enemy. Nectanebus thus manipulated the fortunes of war, for upon the battlefield living men re-enacted to the smallest detail that which the magician had previously decreed with his armies of pawns.

The pseudo-Callisthenes gives many curious details from the life of this extraordinary man. Nectanebus at last departed from Egypt because the gods of that country would no longer render their assistance to his magical operations. He then took up his abode among the Macedonians and in the guise of the god, Ammon, spun the web of sorcery about Alexander the Great, whose claims to a "divine" origin are probably founded upon this circumstance. When the time came for Olympias to give

birth to her son, Nectanebus was present in the role of
an astrologer. Standing beside the queen, he calculated
the positions of the heavenly bodies and besought her

*Horoscope of Alexander the Great*—from Sibly's *Astrology.*

not to permit the child to be born until the most auspicious moment had arrived. "It was not until he saw
a certain splendor in the sky and knew that all the
heavenly bodies were in a favorable position that he

permitted her to bring forth her child."[1] At the birth of Alexander, the earth was shaken, the heavens were filled with fires, and thunders crashed through the deep. At the instant the babe was delivered, Nectanebus exclaimed: "O Queen, now thou wilt give birth to a governor of the world!"

The nobility of Plato's intellect; the estimation in which his writings are held by all civilized peoples; and the significant fact that we are indebted to him for the first allusion to astrology in Greek literature amply justify the publication of his horoscope as a most noble fragment of this ancient learning. Julius Firmicus Maternus calculated the horoscope of this remarkable man in the fourth century of the Christian Era. The scheme of the nativity is given as follows: "If the Ascendant shall be Aquarius, Mars, Mercury, and Venus therein posited; and if Jupiter then be placed in the seventh, having Leo for his sign, and in the second the Sun in Pisces and the Moon in the fifth House, beholding the Ascendant with a trine aspect, and Saturn in the ninth from the Ascendant in Libra; this Geniture renders a Man Interpreter of Divine and heavenly Institutions, who endued with instructive speech, and the power of Divine Wit, and formed in a manner by a celestial Institution, by the true License of disputations shall arrive at all the secrets of Divinity."[2]

The horoscope as set up by Firmicus is extremely probable. The sign in which the sun is placed agrees with Plato's physical appearance, as does the ascendant with the qualities of his mind. Pisces confers heaviness and breadth and "Aristo named him *Plato* (which implieth Latitude) in allusion to the largeness of his

[1] See Budge's *Egyptian Magic.*
[2] See *De Nativitatibus.*

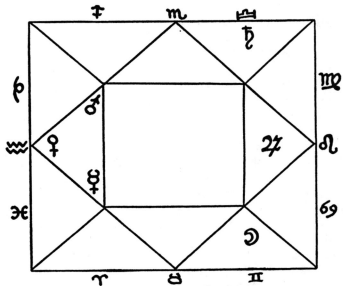

*Horoscope of Plato*—from Julius Firmicus Maternus.

person: others say, to the wideness of his Shoulders."[3]
Neanthes relates the term to the breadth of his forehead. Jupiter, the ruler of Pisces, when powerful, gives
the "divine appearance," and according to Hesychius,
the philosopher was called *Serapis* from the majesty and
dignity of his person. Aquarius has been termed the
sign of the truth-seeker, and of all men it may be said
of Plato that he lived for truth alone. The serenity of
Plato's mind, the earnestness of his endeavor, the synthesis which marks his classification of facts, the humane-
ness and rationality of his soul—all these qualities,
perfected by the magnificent inclusiveness of his erudition, reveal the highly developed Aquarian type.

[3] See Stanley's *History of Philosophy*.

The presence of three planets—Venus, Mercury, and Mars—in the first house bespeaks the particulars of his character. Venus bestows brilliance of speech (his "large eloquence" is mentioned by several authors); comeliness of body ("there was not any imperfection throughout his person"); and also a love of the fine arts. Dicearchus states that he had learned to paint, that he addicted himself to poetry, and the beauty of his words caused it to be said of him that while as a child he lay sleeping the bees made a honeycomb in his mouth. Mercury gives fluency in writing, ability at discourse and argument, and an intensive genius, so that Stanley says of Plato that "he added much to learning and languages by many inventions, as well of things as of words." Plato excelled in geometry, grammar, and rhetoric, creating many terms now used in these sciences. Mars imparts strength of body, love of argument, and courage of conviction. Plato was most proficient in wrestling, and he competed in the Pythian games. In war, it is said that upon at least one occasion "he fought best of all the soldiers."[4] He defended his ideas with great brilliancy and in discourse and debate fearlessly pressed his opinions to their legitimate end. The remainder of the horoscope is equally applicable to the philosopher. Plato died at a most venerable age, "having completed the most perfect number of years, namely, nine multiplied by itself."[5] He was found dead with the books of Sophron lying under his head.

The astrosophy of Plato was a key to the order and procedure of the universe. To him the stars were "divine and eternal animals, ever abiding." In *The Republic* he describes the music of the spheres, the seven planets and

4 See Aristoxenus and Ælian.
5 See Laertius.

also the eighth sphere, which is that of the fixed stars. He also alludes to "the spindle of Necessity on which all the revolutions turn." The whole theory of Platonism is concerned with the descent of the soul through the orbits of the planets and into the sublunar sphere of generation. Once within the embrace of matter, the soul is afflicted by the influences of the stars, and from this affliction it must liberate itself by perfecting the intellect in all matters truly human and divine. The universe is one vast mechanism, dominated by Supreme Intelligence and perpetuating itself through periodic intervals of fertility and sterility. The celebrated passage in *The Timaeus* from which astrologers derive their doctrine of climacterical years relates to the greater apocatastasis which Macrobius calls the grand mundane year, or revolution. "At the same time, however," writes Plato, "it is no less possible to conceive, that the perfect number of time will then accomplish a perfect year, when the celerities of all the eight periods being terminated with reference to each other, shall have a summit, as they are measured by the circle, of that which subsists according to the same and the similar [i.e., according to the sphere of the fixed stars]."[6]

In his commentary on this Platonic doctrine, Proclus observes that the length of the great year is determined by conjunctions of the planets. He notes that the sign of Cancer is the ascendant of the world horoscope and that a period of the universe is that time which must elapse between conjunctions of all the planets in this sign. The vast interval of time between such apocatastases is divisible into a number of lesser periods, each of which resulting from a different harmony of the

[6] See Thomas Taylor's translation.

heavenly bodies is distinguished from the others by the modifications which it causes in the productiveness of nature. "The different periods in which these mutations happen," writes Thomas Taylor, "are called by Plato, with great propriety, periods of *fertility* and *sterility*. For in these periods, a fertility or sterility of men, animals, and plants takes place; so that in fertile periods, mankind will be both more numerous, and upon the whole superior in mental and bodily endowments, to the men of a barren period. And a similar reasoning must be extended to animals and plants. The so much celebrated heroic age was the result of one of these fertile periods, in which men transcending the herd of mankind, both in practical and intellectual virtue, abounded on the earth."[7]

Referring to Plato's universal cycle, Thorndike notes that the statement in *The Tinaeus* "seems to suggest the astrological doctrine of the *magnus annus,* that history begins to repeat itself in every detail when the heavenly bodies have regained their original positions.[8] Aristotle concurs with his master in recognizing the heavenly bodies as superhuman, intelligent, incorporate deities.[9] The interval between this viewpoint and astrology is almost imperceptible; for, according to Diodorus, the Chaldeans taught that "every event in the heavens has its meaning, as part of the eternal scheme of divine forethought." Theophrastus, who succeeded Aristotle in the Peripatetic School, was even more outspoken in his admiration for astrology. Proclus reports him as saying, "The most extraordinary thing of his age was the

[7] See *Theoretic Arithmetic.*
[8] See *History of Magic and Experimental Science.*
[9] See Windelband's *History of Philosophy.*

lore of the Chaldeans, who foretold not only events of public interest but even the lives and deaths of individuals."[10]

Seneca is in accord with the Chaldean Berosus who declared that "whenever all the stars are in conjunction in the sign of Cancer there will be a universal conflagration, and a second deluge when they all unite in Capricorn." (See Thorndike.)

The astral philosophy of the Greeks was most certainly derived from the Asiatics. We cannot do better than to accept Stanley's summary of the origins of Greek learning: "Although some Grecians have challenged to their nation the original of philosophy, yet the more learned of them have acknowledged it derived from the East. To omit the dark traditions of the Athenians concerning Musaeus, of the Thebanes, concerning Linus, and of the Thracians about Orpheus, it is manifest that the original of the Greek philosophy is to be derived from Thales, who travelling into the East, first brought Natural learning, Geometry, and Astrology thence into Greece, for which reason the attribute of Wise was conferred upon him, and at the same time upon six others for their eminence in morality and politics."[11]

[10] See Murray's *Four Stages of Greek Religion*.
[11] See *History of Philosophy*.

# THE ASTROLOGY OF THE ROMANS

*"Fierce Fiery Warriors Fought Upon the Clouds,*
*In Ranks and Squadrons and Right Form of War,*
*Which Drizzled Blood Upon the Capitol. . . .*
*When Beggars Die, There Are No Comets Seen;*
*The Heavens Themselves Blaze Forth the Death of Princes."*
— JULIUS CAESAR.

THE story of the influence of astrology upon the Roman Empire is well nigh a history of Rome itself. The Emperor Numa was addicted to all forms of magical arts. "Marcus Antonius never traveled without an astrologer recommended to him by Cleopatra."[1] Before his ascent to the throne, Augustus Caesar went to the astrologer, Theogenes, who fell on his knees before the youth and predicted his rise to power. Augustus was so impressed that he published his horoscope and had a silver coin struck off with the sign Capricorn under which he was born upon one of its surfaces. The astrologers, Thracyllus, the Elder, and Thracyllus, the Younger, were constantly consulted by both the Emperors Tiberius and Nero. "Tiberius, who believed in nothing else except thunder-storms, placed unbounded faith in the Chaldeans" (astrologers). He had studied the art under Thracyllus, whom he put to a severe test. Tiberius himself reached a high pitch of proficiency. He foretold that Galba would one day reign, and in his last hours revealed the career of his successor, Gaius.[2]

[1] See Blavatsky's *The Secret Doctrine.*
[2] See Granger's *Worship of the Romans.*

According to Seneca, "a meteor 'as big as the moon appeared when Paulus was engaged in the war against Perseus'; similar portents marked the death of Augustus and execution of Sejanus, and gave warning of the death of Germanicus."[3]

Sylla, the astrologer and mathematician, read the horoscope of Caligula, revealing to Caesar the time and conditions under which he would die. This same Emperor was admonished by the Sortes Antiatinae that "he should beware of Cassius," and by the conspiracy and sword of a man of this name he died. Otho surrounded himself with seers and astrologers, and sought advice from Ptolemy, being assured by the latter that he should outlive Nero and be a ruler of the Romans. Nero himself practiced astrology. Vitellius was left upon the horns of a dilemma, he attempted to banish the astrologers from Rome—that is, all except his own—but these "Chaldeans" outwitted him, for they published a proclamation to the effect that the day of their banishment would also be that upon which the Emperor died. Vitellius was so terrified by the prognostication that he permitted them to remain undisturbed. Selenus gave warnings to Vespasian, who consulted his stars daily, Apollonius, the astrologer-magician of Tyana, was also admired and his advice sought by Vespasian, Titus, and Nerva, but viewed with dismay by Nero and Domitian, who were terrified by his wisdom and power. Domitian would make no important move of any kind without consulting his stars.

Adrian, who was an adept in astrology, wrote from the stars a diary of his own life, even predicting the hour of his own death, all this long before the incidents themselves actually occurred. Septimus Severus caused

[3] See Thorndike's *History of Magic and Experimental Science.*

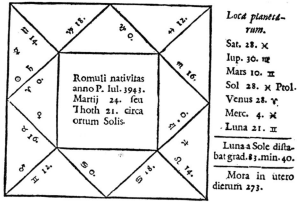

Loca planeta-
rum.

Sat. 28. ♓
Iup. 30. ♍
Mars 10. ♊
Sol 28. ♓ Ptol.
Venus 28. ♈
Merc. 4. ♓
. Luna 21. ♊

Luna a Sole difta-
bat grad. 83. min. 40.

Mora in utero
dierum 273.

*The Horoscope of Romulus.*

his horoscope to be inscribed upon the roof of his judicial palace with the statement of his foreknowledge that
he would not return alive from his expedition to England. He died at York, in accordance with his own
prophetic knowledge. We have already noted that Constantine the Great believed in his stars, and the astrologer, Heliodorus, was the adviser of the Emperor Valens.
Julian, one of the most scholarly of the Roman Emperors,
wrote that in his youth he had been a student of astrology. The historian Ammianus Marcellinus also testifies
to Julian's devotion to the occult sciences.

A curious early writing entitled *Tabulae Frisicae* contains the horoscope of Romulus attributed to Ptolemy.
The rarity of this nativity justifies its publication as an
important fragment of Roman astrology.

Varro, the distinguished Roman scholar, requested
his friend, Lucius Tarutius Firmanus, one of the most
renowned of the Roman astrologers, to cast the horoscope of the Eternal City. With great labor this was

accomplished and Firmanus reported that the walls of
Rome were begun by Romulus in the twenty-second
year of his age, on the eleventh day of the calends of
May, between the second and third hours. At that time,
the sun was in Taurus, the moon in Libra, Saturn in
Scorpio, Jupiter in Pisces, Mars in Scorpio, Venus in
Scorpio, and Mercury in Scorpio. Firmanus, who placed
great reliance in the lunar motion, predicted therefrom
the destiny of Rome. To appreciate the veneration accorded by Romans to those proficient in astrological
lore, we cannot do better than to summarize in the
words of Vitruvius: "Their learning deserves the admiration of mankind."

The Emperor Tiberius had a convenient method of
disposing of *personae non gratae.* High up on a bleak
racky crag on the island of Capri, he had a castle which
could be reached only by a perilous flight of steps on
the edge of a precipice with a sheer drop to the sea.
Anyone suspected of treachery or conspiracy was invited
to an audience with the Emperor in this grim palace.
Visitors were always accompanied in both the ascent
as well as descent by a great Ethiopian slave, who on
their return down, pushed them over the cliff at some
narrow and perilous spot, if their explanations proved
unsatisfactory to Tiberius. A Roman invited to Capri
first made his will and then bade farewell to his friends.
On a a certain day, the astrologer Thracyllus, in obedience to the imperial summons, but fully aware of his
danger, followed the black servant up the tortuous
path. Tiberius received the astrologer very graciously,
discoursing with him at some length upon the merits
of the science.

Thracyllus must have grown uneasy as he received
the imperial confidence that no man ever lived to

betray. The Emperor seemed most impressed and at last inquired in a tone of assumed indifference: "My Thracyllus, do you ever read your own stars?" The astrologer replied that he did. "What, then," continued the Emperor, "do they promise for you in the near future?" It was a critical moment, but Thracyllus was equal to the occasion. He calculated for a few minutes and his face assumed a grave expression. In fact, he became very agitated and, turning to the Emperor, exclaimed in despairing tones: "Sire, my planets warn me that I am in the gravest danger!" The Emperor's face lighted up and he extended his hand to the astrologer. "You are, indeed, a wise man, for I had intended to have you thrown this very night from the rocks of Capri." Thracyllus received many favors from Tiberius, who consulted him frequently thereafter and even studied under the tutelage of this gifted diviner.

The eclectic spirit prevailing in Rome caused the Eternal City to become a mart for the exchange of ideas —religious, philosophic, and political. The temples of various gods were clustered together in the Forum. In this cosmopolitan atmosphere astrology gained many converts among the powerful, the wealthy, and the wise. Several new titles were bestowed upon the star-gazers. They were called *Astrologi, Mathematici,* and *Genethliaci.* The origin of the science caused those proficient in it also to be termed *Chaldaei,* or *Babylonii.* In writings of this period, therefore, astrologers of all nationalities were known as *Chaldeans,* and are so denominated by Hippolytus, who makes grudging reference to their abilities. "Under the wisest Emperors, Rome had a School of Astrology, wherein were secretly taught the occult influences of the Sun, Moon, and Saturn."[4] Even

4 Quoted by H. P. Blavatsky in *The Secret Doctrine.*

when the astrologers fell upon evil times, they continued to flourish and "the penalty of death decreed nearly everywhere against those mathematicians (astrologers) who happened to predict falsely diminished neither their number nor their tranquillity of mind."[5]

We also learn that "The Emperor Hadrian, who assigned great importance to the influence of the sky and the stars, erected a superb building at Jerusalem (which he called Ælia, a name derived from the sun and his own, Ælius), which was called Dodecapylon, or the temple with twelve gates, an evident allusion to the twelve houses of the sun. He also divided the town into seven portions—a division which had relation to the number of planets and of the planetary spheres. The new Jerusalem of the Apocalypse has also twelve gates, twelve foundations, and twelve angels at each gate. It was astrology which developed the plan of this visionary city, just as it inspired the plan of the new city built by Hadrian."[6]

Though Hadrian applied himself to astrology and magical arts in order to enjoy the extensions of knowledge they bestowed, he sought at the same time to prevent others from benefiting their fortunes by applying themselves to such sciences. It is now generally conceded that it was by the aid of the prophetic waters of the Kastalian spring that Hadrian came to the imperial chair. "We may recall," writes W. R. Halliday, "the attitude of the Roman Emperors toward astrology. If the stars merely reveal the future, what harm could the astrologer effect? Yet to prophesy the Emperor's death was a capital offense. [Queen Elizabeth caused similar legislation in England.] Hadrian is said to have blocked

[5] Ibid.
[6] See *Mankind: Their Origin and Destiny.*

up the Kastalian spring, because he had learned his imperial destiny from its prophetic water, and feared that others might consult it for a similar purpose."[7]

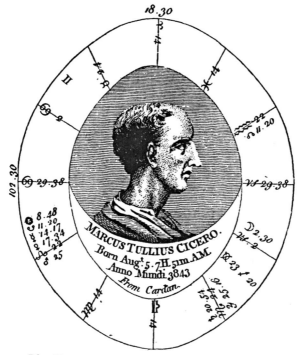

*The Horoscope of Cicero*—from Sibly's *Astrology.*

The Emperor Julian confesses his addiction to "almost every form of pagan divination." In his *Oration to the Sovereign Sun,* this worthy Roman—of whom it has been said that he is called an apostate because he

[7] See *Greek Divination.*

would not be one—declares the sun "from his middle order between the planets" to be the chief among the *Intellectual Gods*. He even invokes to his aid the famous words of Aristotle that "man and the sun generate man." Julian then supplicates Mercury, whom he terms "the ruling deity of discourse," and writes at some length upon the heavenly harmony: As the sun quadruply divides these three worlds [empyreal, ethereal, and material] on account of the communion of the zodiac with each, so he again divides the zodiac into twelve powers of gods, and each of these into three others so that thirty-six are produced in the whole [the decans of Ptolemy]. Hence, as it appears to me, a triple benefit of the Graces proceeds to us from the heavens." After Julian became Emperor, we can well understand from the nature of the man himself why he proposed that the Kastalian spring be unblocked so that its prophetic waters might again contribute to the well-being of the state. Julian is supposed to have said of the oracles of Apollo that through their agency, the greater part of civilization had come into being in that they had revealed the will of the gods in matters both religious and political, and had wisely regulated such states as would accept their advisements.

In their extremely superficial examination of astrological phenomena, modern psychologists have attempted to explain away the science by maintaining that predictions bring about their own fulfillment. But here again is a dilemma. Take, for example, the story of the Greek tragic poet, Æschylus who, discovering from his stars that he would die at a certain time by an object falling upon him, sought to escape his destiny by remaining in the desert until after the fatal aspect had passed. Seating himself in an open place, with nothing but the blue sky above him, Æschylus felt himself reasonably secure. But a great bird, mistaking the poet's bald head for a rock, dropped a turtle upon it to break its shell, thereby killing Æschylus and fulfilling the prediction.

*The Horoscope of Nero Caesar*—from Sibly's *Astrology*.

Other similar cases are recorded in which the stars have vindicated themselves in extraordinary ways. Michael Scott, the astrologer and confidant of Emperor Frederick the Second, predicted that he himself would die from a rock hitting him upon the head. Scott was killed while at prayer by a loose stone that fell from the roof of the cathedral where he was kneeling in prayer. Franciscus Junctinus, a Florentine astrologer, predicted for himself a violent death, and upon the very hour foretold was killed while sitting in his library by some heavy books falling upon him from an upper shelf. No more dramatic incident is recorded in the history of Rome than the interview between Agrippina, the mother of Nero, and the Chaldean astrologer. This contriving woman sought the advice of the stars as to the outcome of her life's ambition to make her son the Emperor of the Romans. The astrologer cast the nativity and rendered the following judgment: "If he reigns, he shall kill his mother." Without a moment's hesitation, Agrippina, with set teeth, hissed back the answer: "Let him kill me so that he but reigns!" Needless to state, the stars gave honest judgment. In later years, Nero surrounded himself with astrologers, and Bamilus was not only his constant adviser but repeatedly warned the Emperor that his reckless course was bringing him to an untimely end.

No consideration of astrology during the Roman period should omit reference to the opinions of the Alexandrian Neo-Platonists, who included among their number some of the wisest men of all time. Of the Alexandrian Platonists, Plotinus and Proclus are preeminent. Porphyry and Iamblichus also merit mention. According to Plotinus, "it is abundantly evident . . . that the motion of the heavens affects things on earth."[8] Golden-souled Proclus, surnamed the Platonic Successor, who succeeded Syrianus in the rectorship of the Platonic school at Athens, wrote a paraphrase of Ptol-

[8] See Thorndike's *History of Magic and Experimental Science.*

emy's *Tetrabiblos*, which was so excellent that Melanchthon found it worthy of edit, although but the previous year he had republished Camerarius' edition of the same work with original emendations.[9] Proclus also prepared several commentaries upon the astronomical and astrological precepts of Ptolemy, which amply set forth his attitude upon such matters. Iamblichus defends astrology against the stigma of fatalism by showing that only the animal soul of man is subjected to the sidereal influence, and Porphyry in a letter to Anebo declares that the articifers of efficacious images should not be despised "for they observe the motion of celestial bodies.[10] Porphyry tells us that when he had resolved to kill himself, Plotinus read his intentions in the stars and dissuaded him from so doing.[11]

[9] See preface to Ashmand's edition of Ptolemy's *Tetrabiblos*.
[10] See Thorndike's *History of Magic and Experimental Science*.
[11] See *Unheard-of Curiosities*, etc.

# THE ASTROLOGY OF THE AZTECS

*"Before Undertaking a Magical Act the NAUALLI Consulted His TONALAMATL and Satisfied Himself that the Astrological Omens Were Favorable. He Then Applied Himself to the Study of the Ritual Procedure. . . . These Preliminary Steps Accomplished, He Next Betook Himself to a Desert Place, and Called Upon One or Other of the Presiding Deities of Magic, and Possibly the God of the Hour, for Assistance in His Task."—LEWIS SPENCE.*

THERE is abundant evidence in the hieroglyphical figures of the Mexican Indians, and the commentaries thereon by the early Spanish fathers, that the several aboriginal civilizations of Central America developed elaborate systems of natal and judicial astrology. Prescott, in his *History of the Conquest of Mexico*, notes that the Aztec Indians, when a child was born into their nation, instantly summoned an astrologer (adivino) whose duty it was to ascertain the destiny of the newborn babe. "The sign," writes Lucien Biart, "that marked the day of his birth was noted, and also the one that ruled during the period of the last thirteen years. If the child was born at midnight, they compared the preceding day and the day following."[1] Like the Greeks, Egyptians and other ancient peoples, the augurs among the Mexicans foretold events from the positions of the planets, the arrangements of sacred numbers, from clouds, storms, eclipses, comets, the flight of birds, and the actions of animals.

Their astrological knowledge was derived principally

[1] See *The Aztecs*.

from the doctrines and revelations of Quetzalcoatl, the first and foremost of their philosophers and teachers. Quetzalcoatl was the Son of Heaven; his true parent was the Universal Creator in the dual aspect of father-mother. In the physical world he was born of the Virgin Sochiquetzal and his coming was annunciated by a heavenly apparition which declared that it had come as an ambassador from the god of the Milky Way to discover among mortals the blessed Virgin who was to become the mother of the Divine Incarnation. Among the appellations of the god Quetzalcoatl, therefore, are "He who was born of the Virgin," "Lord of the Winds," and "priest-prophet-king." The astrology of the Aztecs was thus derived from the highest authority, and we learn that from Quetzalcoatl the knowledge of the starry science descended through a sacerdotal line of initiated priest-philosophers. Quetzalcoatl himself devised the astrological cycle and the Tonalamatl—the Book of the Fates of Men.

The Spanish writer, Mendietam, gives a brief description of the manner in which Quetzalcoatl came to originate the sacred astrological calendar. "He says that the gods thought it well that the people should have some means of writing by which they might direct themselves, and two of their number, Oxomoco and Cipactonal, who dwelt in a cave in Cuernavaca, especially considered the matter. Cipactonal thought that her descendent Quetzalcoatl should be consulted, and she called him into counsel. He too, thought the idea of the calendar good, and the three addressed themselves to the task of making the *Tonalamatl,* or Book of Fate. To Cipactonal was given the privilege of choosing and writing the first sign, or day-symbol of the calendar. She painted the

*Cipactli* or dragon animal, and called the sign *Ce Cipactli* ("one *Cipactli*"). Oxomoco then wrote *Om Acatl* ("two canes") and Quetzalcoatl "three houses" and so on, until the thirteen signs were completed."[2]

In ancient Mexico, as in other parts of the civilized world, astrology was cultivated not by the ignorant and superstitious but by the great and learned. Three of the great names in the whole history of the Aztec nation are intimately connected with this science—Quetzalcoatl, Nazahualpilli, and Montezuma. We have already mentioned Quetzalcoatl as the highest of all authorities in the arts and sciences of these people. Nazahualpilli was the king of Tezcuco. Of this king Torquemada writes in the second book of the *Indian Monarchy*, "They say that he was a great astrologer, and prided himself much on his knowledge of the motions of the celestial bodies; and being attached to this study, that he caused inquiries to be made throughout the entire of his dominions, for all such persons as were at all conversant with it, whom he brought to his court, and imparted to them whatever he knew; and ascending by night on the terraced roof of his palace, he thence considered the stars, and disputed with them on all difficult questions concerned with them. I at least can affirm that I have seen a place on the outside of the roof of the palace, enclosed within four walls only a yard in height, and just of sufficient breadth for a man to lie down in; in each angle of which was a hole of perforation, in which was placed a lance, upon which was hung a sphere; and on by inquiring the use of this square space, a grandson of his, who was showing me the palace, replied that it was for King Nazahualpilli, when he

[2] See Lewis Spence.

went by night attended by his astrologers to contemplate the heavens and the stars; whence I inferred that what was reported of him is true; and I think that the reason of the walls being elevated one yard above the terrace, and a sphere of cotton or silk being hung from the poles was for the sake of measuring more accurately the celestial motions."

Lord Kingsborough, the author of the greatest of all works on Mexican antiquities, in commenting on the astronomical knowledge of the Mexicans, says that it can hardly be doubted that these Indians were acquainted with many scientific instruments. The thirteenth plate of Dupaix's *The Monuments of New Spain* reproduces an ancient figure representing a man holding something resembling a telescope to one of his eyes. It was King Nazahualpilli who stood before Montezuma when that young man ascended to the throne of Mexico and congratulated the whole nation on the election of a king "whose deep knowledge of heavenly things insured to his subjects his comprehension of those of an earthly nature."[3]

Montezuma was the outstanding organizing genius of the Aztec world. We see from the old codices (books) that he conquered forty-four cities, binding them to his rule so that they paid tribute to him and acknowledged vassalage. This last king of the Indians was not only a great general, statesman and prince, but also a distinguished patron of the occult arts, especially astrology. The interpreter of the *Collection of Mendoza* writes that he "was by nature wise, an astrologer and philosopher and skilled and generally versed in all the arts, both in those of the military, as well as those of a civil

[3] See *Antiquities of Mexico.*

nature, and from his extreme gravity and state, the monarchy under his sway began to verge towards empire." He enforced the laws and statutes of his predecessors "and being endowed with so much wisdom, he by the excellence of his own understanding" established such new laws and ordinances as would perfect and complete the older ones. The Spanish conquest of Mexico is in no way a reflection upon the wisdom and integrity of Montezuma. It has well been said, "the Aztecs were not conquered by Spaniards but by horses." This animal, unknown to the Indians, was a demoralizing force utterly beyond their experience. Furthermore the high integrity and honor of Montezuma made it impossible for him to cope successfully with the Conquistadores who were utterly wanting in any vestige of principle. Horses, guns and infamy spurred on by greed wrought the ruin of the Aztec nation and the death of Montezuma in the fifty-third year of his age.[4]

Nor did King Nazahualpilli fail to warn Montezuma of the tragedy that was to befall his empire. The wise old astrologer revealed to the emperor that within a few years his cities would be destroyed and his vassals decimated, further declaring that celestial signs and other phenomena would verify his predictions and announce the end of the old Mexican civilization. Mendieta says that prophecies were current four generations before the coming of the Spaniards to the effect that bearded men with sharp swords, strange garments and "caskets" on their heads would arrive from across the sea, destroy the Aztec gods and conquer their lands. The evil omens which Nazahualpilli had described came to pass. The stars in their courses wrought the downfall of Mexico.

4 See *Antiquities of Mexico.*

In 1505 there was a famine. In the first year of the new cycle, which began in 1507 there was an eclipse—a most evil indication, according to the star-gazers. This, naturally, was followed by an earthquake and later by military reverses.

Each succeeding year, according to Bancroft, "confirmed their apprehensions by one or more signs or occurrence of an ominous nature."[5] Not long after the earthquake, there appeared in broad daylight a comet with three heads, speeding eastward and seeming to shake sparks from its tail. In harmony with the laws of mundane astrology this comet was regarded as a harbinger of doom. In 1509 "a pyramidal light, which scattered sparks on all sides, rose at midnight from the eastern horizon till the apex reached the zenith, where it faded at dawn."[6] This phenomenon continued for forty days causing a panic among the people and grave anxiety among the astrologers who realized that the end was fast approaching. They circulated statements to the effect that the light presaged "wars, famine, pestilence, mortality among the lords," in fact, every imaginable ill. In dismay Montezuma sent for the learned Nazahualpilli, who confirmed the evil readings of the other astrologers and discovering from his own horoscope that the calamity should descend upon himself with the rest, retired with philosophical stoicism to await the end and prepare for death. The last of the evil signs appeared in 1519, the very year in which the Spaniards arrived. An awe-inspiring comet hung over the City of Mexico for several days like the fiery sword that Josephus describes as hovering above Jerusalem just prior to its destruc-

[5] See Bancroft's *History of the Pacific States of North America*.
[6] See Sahagun's *Historia de la Conquista de Mexico*.

tion. Montezuma made peace with his gods and allowed his enemies to enter the valley of Anahuac unmolested.

A few observations from Stuart Chase relating to the astronomical knowledge of the ancient Americans may not be out of place. "In astronomy the American mind reached its climax, and the Mayas were its high priests. Starting, as we have seen, with observations of the heavens some 4,000 years ago, the Maya calendar was developed to a point where it was possible to distinguish without duplication any given day in 370,000 years! This was far in advance of European astronomy; more accurate than anything socalled western civilization achieved until very recent times." In another place this author continues: "The Aztecs borrowed the Maya principles but never achieved such mathematical elegance. Their solar calendar, however, was more accurate than that of the Spaniards. They were found in full knowledge of the year of Venus, eclipses, solstices, equinoxes, and such phenomena." Speaking of the culture of the central Americans Mr. Chase observes: "is it unreasonable to suppose that, during these 150 years, [450 to 600 A. D.] the Mayas were the most civilized people on the planet?"[7]

The astrological systems of the Aztecs and the nations of Central America and Yucatan are evidently identical in origin, with that of the Mayans, differing only in minor details from those of the more northern Indians. Alexander von Humboldt, an authority on these subjects, has pointed out the numerous correspondences which exist between the astrological symbols of the Mexicans and those of the Chaldeans, Greeks and Egyp-

[7] See *Mexico, A Study of Two Americas.*

tians. Though present knowledge of Aztec metaphysics is extremely fragmentary, one may dimly perceive something of the vastness and profundity of their theories. It may yet be demonstrated that their knowledge of the occult forces working in nature was scarcely less complete than that of the Eastern hemisphere. The Indians assigned special virtues to the hours, days, weeks, months, years, and other greater cycles of 52 years which they termed "bundles." Each of the hours of the day and night had a god which ruled over it. The day cycle consisted of 13 hours, the 7th hour being noon, so that the number 7 was regarded with special veneration. The gods ruling over the diurnal period are elaborately pictured in the Aztec books and are termed collectively the Lords of the Day. The Aztec night consisted of 9 periods, the 5th period being midnight so that the numeral 5 was accepted as an evil symbol. The Spaniards referred to the nine nocturnal divinities as "Senores de las Noches"—Lords of the Night. We learn also that the various hours of both day and night were demonstrated as good, bad and indifferent. To the Aztec astrologers, to be born in the first hour of the night was fortunate, the second hour unfortunate, the third hour fortunate again, the fourth hour indifferent, and so forth. These Lords of the Day and Night correspond with the planetary hour deities of the Chaldeans.

From this point we must proceed to an analysis of the Tonalamatl, the Book of Good and Bad Days or of Fate, in which is set forth a perpetual calendar of benefic and malefic periods. This work was not only consulted at the birth of the child but was also used as a textbook of electional astrology from which was determined auspicious periods for the commencement of enterprises for the accomplishment of any desired end. The Tonal-amatl combines in one volume cosmogony and divina-tion, a circumstance which has induced modern writers on the subject of the Aztec civilization to admit that an understanding of this book is essential to an apprecia-tion of the arts, philosophies and sciences of these In-dians.

The Tonalamatl in the *Aubin Collection* is a rare and excellent example of the sacred divinatory system. The book contains 20 leaves upon each of which is con-spicuously represented 13 figures. In addition to these are other figures representing the Lords of the Day and Night, bringing the entire total to 52; upon each leaf is also a larger key figure representing the deity ruling over the time period set forth upon and by the page. The Aztecs had both a judicial and a sacred year. The judicial year consisted of 365 days and was arranged in 18 months of 20 days each and five inter-calendary days which were nameless and unfortunate. No man per-formed labor which could be avoided upon these five days; to be born upon one of them was a disaster and men began no enterprise upon them lest it fail. 52 of these 365-day years constituted a cycle, and it is now believed that although the Mayans carried their time calculations into vast cycles of time, the Aztecs had no method of chronology beyond the 52-year cycle.

The sacred year, the one set forth in the Tonala-matl of Quetzalcoatl, consisted of but 260 days. These were divided into 20 periods of 13 days each. These 20 periods were conveniently, if incorrectly, termed months. Seventy-three of these sacred years of 260 days each were equal to 52 years of the 365-day years, and thus the two calendars were reconciled. The Tonal-

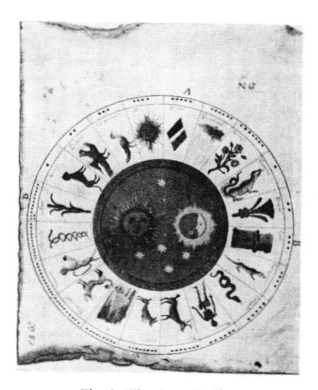

Fig. 1. The Aztec Zodiac

culque, the astrologers who used the Book of Good and Bad Days, worked with a zodiac composed of the 20-month signs, arranged as in Figure 1, which is reproduced from a manuscript in the Museo de Nacional de Mexico. Each of the months containing 13 days begins with the 14th sign from that of the previous month and the 13 days of each month proceed in order from the sign ruling the month itself.

The Zodiac begins on the upper right side of the wheel where the single dot appears in the outer circle, so that the first sign is the Crocodile. It then proceeds clockwise in the order of the dots, and reaching 13 begins with 1 again and continues on to 7. The dots here form a key to the cycles, for if a given month begins with the Crocodile and continues for 13 days it will end in the sign marked D (left center). The next month will then begin in the sign following that, here marked 1 (left center) and shown by a Jaguar, will then continue in a clockwise direction for 13, ending in the sign of the Skeleton (lower right). The next month will begin with the Deer, the sign directly following the Skeleton, and continue clockwise in this manner until 20 such cycles of 13 days have been completed when it will be evident that the count will return to the starting point—the Crocodile. This constitutes the Tonalamatl cycle. Each of the months of 13 days is under the general control of the deity and virtue which rules its first day or beginning, and the other 12 days of that month are modifications of this first influence. This procedure is somewhat similar to the decan theory and minor divisions of astrological signs used by the Egyptians and Hindus.

The 20 signs of the Zodiac with their Aztec names and English equivalents are as follows:

| | | |
|---|---|---|
| 1. | Cipactli | The Crocodile. |
| 2. | Eecatl | The Wind. |
| 3. | Calli | The House. |
| 4. | Cuelzpalin | The Lizard. |
| 5. | Couatl | The Snake. |
| 6. | Miquiztli | Death. |
| 7. | Macatl | The Deer. |
| 8. | Tochtli | The Rabbit. |
| 9. | Atl | The Water. |
| 10. | Itzcuintli | The Dog. |
| 11. | Ocomatli | The Ape. |
| 12. | Malinalli | The Twisted. |
| 13. | Acatl | The Reed. |
| 14. | Ocelotl | The Jaguar. |
| 15. | Quauhtli | The Vulture. |
| 16. | Cozcaquauhili | The Eagle. |
| 17. | Olin | Motion (the Sun). |
| 18. | Tecpatl | The Flint Knife. |
| 19. | Quiauitl | The Rain. |
| 20. | Xochitl | The Flower. |

In the center of the calendar will be noted the Sun, Moon and five stars. Among the Aztec deities are six which they call the Wanderers and for whom no satisfactory explanation has yet been advanced. The word planet signifying wanderer, we may infer that these gods were connected with the planets. As Jupiter is the sacred planet for the time cycles of the Tibetans, so Venus, the star of Quetzalcoatl, is the sacred planet of the time cycles of the Mexicans. The Mayans of the more southern latitudes also observed the time cycle of Mars. Figure 2 is a reproduction of page 75 of the *Vatican Codex* of the Mexicans and depicts the Tonalamatl cycle in the

Fig. 2. The Macrocosmic Man

form of a Macrocosmic Man. The design is startlingly reminiscent of the familiar cut-up man of the medieval almanac makers. The figure is doubly instructive. First it shows the hieroglyphics for the Zodiacal signs but their order does not correspond with that of the natural calendar. No. 1. is the Deer. 2. the Crocodile. 3. the Flower. 4. Motion, the Sun, and Earthquake. 5. the Eagle. 6. the Vulture. 7. the Water. 8. the House. 9. Death, Skull. 10. the Rain. 11. the Dog. 12. the Rabbit. 13. the Flint Knife. 14. the Wind. 15. the Ape. 16. the Reed. 17. the Twisted. 18. the Lizard. 19. the Jaguar. 20. the Snake.

In the explanation of the *Codex Vaticanus*, it is written that the Aztecs assigned the 20 letters or figures of their cycle, which they employed in all their calculations, to the various parts of the human body, and cured by a knowledge of the astrological virtues of the signs those who became ill or suffered pains in the various members. The sign of the Crocodile was assigned to the liver; the Flower to the breast; Motion, the Sun, to the tongue; the Eagle to the right arm; the Vulture to the right ear; the Flint Knife to the teeth; the Wind to the breath; the Monkey to the left arm; the Reed to the heart; the Twisted Herbs to the bowels; the Lizard to the womb of woman; the Jaguar to the left foot; and the Serpent to the male organ of generation. They regarded the serpent, as did most ancient peoples, as the symbol of both wisdom and sin, possibly deriving from the Orientals a knowledge of the twofold significance of the serpent power. Our author writes of the significance of this Zodiacal Man: "Even still physicians continue to use this figure when they perform cures; and according to the sign and hour in which the patient became ill, they examine whether the disease corresponds with the ruling sign; from which it is plain that this nation is not as brutal as some persons pretend, [!] since they observed so much method and order in their affairs and employed the same means as our astrologers and physicians use, as this figure still obtains amongst them, and may be found in their repertories."

From the above we gain an introduction to the medical astrology of the Aztecs. Throughout available writings are scattered hints as to the readings of the various signs, thus the Lizard signifies both fecundity and incontinence; the Skull or Skeleton, death; the Deer, drought and famine; Water, the vicissitudes of life; the Dog, fire and sharpness; the Ape, dancing, sport, pleasure; the Reed, judicial power, governorship; the Jaguar, darkness and evil; the Eagle, war; the Vulture, old age and decrepitude; Rain, evil outbursts in the air; the Flower, the heart, the flow of blood. The four signs of the Reed, the Rabbit, the House and the Flint Knife correspond to the equinoctial and solstitial signs of our present astrology and signify the four ages which constantly dominate the year and all its cycles.

The cosmological aspect of Aztec astrology is a great subject in itself but we learn from the fragments of the old lore that the creation, maintenance and final dissolution of the universe is according to a certain order of these Tonalamatl symbols.

# THE ASTROLOGY OF THE ARABIANS

*"Astrology Is Based on the Principle That All the Changes Oc-*
*curring in the Sublunary World, i.e., the Aristotelian 'Generation*
*and Corruption' Are Intimately Connected with the Particular*
*Nature and the Movements of the Celestial Bodies."*—ENCYCLO-
PAEDIA OF ISLAM.

THE arts and sciences have always flourished under the
Star and Crescent of Islam. The Arabs possessed an extraordinary capacity for scholarship, and, like the Chinese, established their social and cultural systems upon
the solid foundation of knowledge. During the Middle
Ages a theological blight descended upon the greater
part of Christendom; a pest of priests stripped the occidental countries of practically every vestige of classical
learning. Europe continued for centuries in an unbe-
lievable state of superstition and ignorance. Arrogant
princes and an ambitious clergy conspired together to
the common woe. It was not until the Moorish conquests
of Spain that knowledge, culture and progress regained
ascendancy over the selfishness of petty nobles and the
bigotry of ecclesiastics. From all parts of Europe men
athirst for learning, and long denied that mental im-
provement which is indispensable to the well-being of
the soul, flocked to the universities of the Moors. Re-
turning in due time to their own countries, these scholars established schools and clinics for the further
dissemination of art, philosophy and science.

It was from the Moorish professors of Toledo that
Gerard of Cremona secured the famous *Canon* of Avi-

cenna which became the great astro-medical textbook of Europe. Men will go to great ends to become wise, and there is an account that Abelard of Bath disguised himself as a Mohammedan student and, journeying to the College of Cordova, obtained from the Arabic masters there a copy of Euclid's *Elements*, which he translated, and which gained wide circulation during the fourteenth and fifteenth centuries. Astrology, which had conquered Italy a thousand years earlier, had its triumphant re-entry into Europe with the Moors. It permeated their scientific books and was accepted as an essential part of their curriculums. From Spain astrology spread first to one country then to another until the science, with all its Arabic involvements and complications, came to be generally recognized and was accorded a high place in many centers of learning.

The numerous and splendid princes of Arabia were for the most part patrons of education and culture. They spent vast fortunes in the accumulation of libraries, and sent scholars to all parts of the world in search of knowledge. They erected observatories, developed optics, and compiled catalogs of the stars. It is said of Al-Mansur, founder of Bagdad, that when he had conquered the army of the Greek Emperor Michael III, he asked no spoils of victory beyond copies of the scientific and philosophical books of the best Greek authors.[1] The celebrated Caliph Al-Raschid, second only to Solomon in glory and in wisdom, was given to the occult arts, and the stories of the *Thousand and One Nights* abound with references to astrology and astromancy. From the tales of Scheherazade we discover the honor and dignity accorded to the starry science by noble and commoner alike. Al-Mamun, the distinguished son of the illustri-

[1] See *Regilding the Crescent*, by F. G. Aflafo.

ous Al-Raschid, ordered the astronomical and astrological books of Ptolemy to be translated into Arabic, and it is now generally accepted that the Caliph—"a man profoundly versed in literature and science"—was personally addicted to astrology and frequently employed it in administering grave problems of state.

We have already referred to the important part played by astrology in the rise of the Ottoman Empire. The English astrologer Raphael gives several examples of predictions made and advices given to the Emperors of this house. Raphael sums up his historical review of astrology and magic in Islam as follows: "Hence these sciences were circulated amongst the different Arabian tribes, by whom they were much respected as in Egypt; indeed the respect entertained for them by the Arabians in general, contributed in a great degree to the success of Mohammed. In his life we see the favorable predictions of many very celebrated Astrologers of his time; and among others, that of *Eukeaz*, who told the uncle of the 'Prophet,' that all circumstances in his infancy conspired to announce that he would be a very extraordinary man, and that his life should be guarded with the most vigilant attention. As also the prediction of another, no less famous in the art, who on being presented to him at Bassora, took Mohammed by the hand, and exclaimed with transport, *'Behold the Lord of the World, the Mercy of the Universe.'"*[2]

It seems most appropriate to insert at this point the horoscope of Mohammed, Prophet of Islam, the "Desired of all Nations." The chart is set according to the Oriental method and tradition and is reproduced from the writings of Professor B. Suryanarain Row.[3] The

[2] See Raphael's *Manual of Astrology.*
[3] See *Royal Horoscopes.*

birth time of the Prophet is recorded as Monday, April 20th, A. D. 571, 1 hour 25 minutes and 35 seconds A. M., at Mecca.

In his interpretation of the chart, Dr. Row ascribes the eloquence and fire which this great leader possessed to the conjunction of Jupiter and Saturn in the eleventh house. He also declares that the Dragon's Tail in the twelfth house "shows his advanced gnana or divine wis-

| Venus<br><br>Mercury | Sun<br><br>Mars | | Rahu |
|---|---|---|---|
| <br><br>Birth<br>20 | RASEE DIAGRAM | | |
| Kethu | Saturn<br><br>Jupiter | Moon | |

*The Horoscope of Mohammed.*

dom, and the final emancipation, he obtained by his great wisdom and internal development."

Translated into English, but not recalculated into the western form, the Hindu chart of Mohammed consists of the following elements: Capricorn is ascending; Venus and Mercury are in Pisces; the Sun and Mars in Aries; the Dragon's Head in Gemini and the Dragon's Tail in Sagittarius; the Moon in Libra, opposed to the

Sun; Jupiter and Saturn are in Scorpio; Saturn, being the lord of the Ascendant, is with Jupiter, a very favorable sign for power and public recognition.

The astrology of the Arabs was derived from numerous and widely separated sources. It is generally accepted that its Grecian background was derived principally from Ptolemy, Vettius Valens, Dorotheus Sidonius, Teucer, and Antiochus. A considerable part was also drawn from Pahlawi and Indian books and from the oral traditions of Mesopotamia, Syria and Egypt.[4] In their astrological philosophy the Muslim peoples are essentially eclectic. All tradition was their province, but in one particular they departed from the older systems. They perfected the mathematical aspect of astrology, achieving a high degree of accuracy in spherical trigonometry and other advanced mathematical sciences. The Arabs also devised numerous tables for the calculation of nativities and reduced a vast astrological lore to an orderly and systematic procedure. They formulated many of the terms now used in astrological literature, creating a considerable vocabulary to distinguish the nomenclature of this science from that of other forms of learning. The Arabian astrologers became proficient not only in natal astrology but in predictions relating to cities, races, religions and other mundane, horary and electional subjects. Predictions were successfully made from eclipses of the sun and moon, comets, and other celestial phenomena.

The technical name for astrology with the Muslims is "The Science of the Decrees of the Stars." The astrologer is called Ah-Kami or Munadjdjim, the latter name also signifying an astronomer. Not until the nineteenth century A. D. was any precise distinction made between

---

[4] See *Encyclopaedia of Islam:* Article: Astrology.

an astronomer and an astrologer and each was presumed to possess the knowledge peculiar to the other.[5] The Arabs recognized the importance of astrology in physiology and medicine. In this they accepted the opinions of Hippocrates and developed a considerable science of planetary cycles, climacterical periods and critical days. The opinions of the Arabs in these matters are preserved for European astrologers in Culpeper's *Semeiotica Uranica*. This noted astrologer, physician and herbalist derives much of the contents of this work from the treatise of the Arabian physician Abraham Avenezra on *Critical Days*.

An interesting sidelight on Arabian astrology is the prediction relative to the birth and rise of Genghis Khan and the Tartar conquest of the world, as quoted by Sepharial, the English astrologer:

"Prof. Browne, the learned author of a translation of the Chahar Maqala, or 'Four Discourses of Nizami-i-Arudi, of Samarcand,' gives a prophetic poem attributed to Avicenna (Ibn Sina), in which the Tartar invasion is foretold from a conjunction of Saturn and Jupiter in the sign of Capricorn. Ibn Abi Usaybia also mentions another poem on the same subject by the same author, and which he says was recited to him by a Persian merchant, which begins: 'When Mars arises from the land of Babylon, and the two unlucky planets are in conjunction, then Beware! Beware! there must be then needs happen great things and needs must the Tartars come to your country.' The conjunction of Saturn and Jupiter referred to in the prophecy must have been that of the year A. D. 984, which was the only one during the life of Avicenna which happened in Capricorn. For Avicenna was born in August A. D. 980, and died in

5 See *Encyclopaedia of Islam:* Article: Astrology.

**1037.** The 'two unlucky planets' are of course Mars and Saturn, but there is no mention of the date or sign of conjunction, so that this rather frequent phenomenon cannot be fixed. I am interested more especially with the conjunction of the great planets Saturn and Jupiter, and can only conclude that Avicenna must have had access to records which showed that the conjunction took place about four years after his birth. The poet-astrologer would no doubt seize upon this as a configuration of primary political importance, and would use his faculty towards an interpretation of its symbolism, with, as the course of history shows, remarkable accuracy. In the course of his letter, Prof. Browne calls attention to a prediction by the Persian poet Anwari, 'who foretold a great tempest on the occasion of the conjunction of five planets in the sign of the Balance, on 29 Jumada II, in the year 582 A. H., equal to the 16th of September A. D. 1186. The night happened to be exceptionally calm, and Anwari was overwhelmed with ridicule for his forecast; but it was afterwards noted that Genghis Khan, the chief of the devastating Tartars, was born on that night, and it was considered that Anwari foresaw a great storm but misunderstood its nature.'

"This is interesting. I find that on the 16th of September the Sun was in Libra 0:25 at midnight in the said year, the Moon was just two days past the conjunction and still in the sign Libra, its longitude being 29:14; Saturn was in Libra, its longitude being 5:20; Jupiter in Libra 1:02; Mars in Libra 10:04; and thus there were 'five planets in the sign of the Balance.' Uranus was in Taurus 24:46, Mercury in Virgo 15:35, and Venus in Virgo 16:26. In Blair's *Chronology* I find an entry: '1186—The great conjunction of the Sun and all the planets happened this year on the 14th of September.'

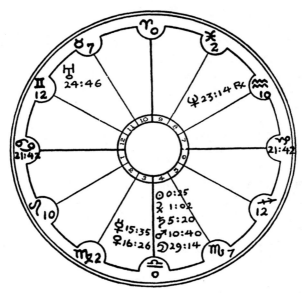

*The Horoscope of Genghis Khan.*

The new Moon of the 14th being close to Saturn, Jupiter, and Mars would have been a striking spectacle if it
could have been seen, and the Persian astrologer-poet
was justified in predicting a 'great tempest.' "[6]

From the above notes by Sepharial we have constructed an approximate horoscope for the Great Khan.
The astonishing conjunction of planets in the sign of
Libra well testifies to the extraordinary genius of the
great Mongol, who, rising from obscurity and, without
benefit of any educational opportunities, became one of
the greatest organizers, military geniuses and political
powers that the world has ever known—a Man of Destiny. The histories of Genghis Khan for the most part

[6] See *British Astrological Journal.*

ignore the occult aspects of his career. The Khan came into power at the beginning of the thirteenth century, at which time Europe was awaiting the Millenium and the Second Advent of Christ was expected.

Genghis Khan was called the son of the Sun and Moon, and the empire which he founded was named the Wise Government or the Government of Wisdom. The title which the great Khan bore was that of the Emperor of all Men, and the Mongols believed that he had been produced by a miracle, that through him God might punish mankind for the sins that had been committed in the names of religion and justice. The mother of Genghis Khan declared him to be the son of the Light of Heaven. Ranking, in his *Historical Researches into Mexico,* thus describes the birth of the Kha Khan: "His mother having been left a widow, lived a retired life: but some time after the death of her husband Douyan-Byan, she was suspected to be pregnant. The deceased husband's relatives forced her to appear before the chief judge of the tribe, for this crime. She boldly defended herself, by declaring that no man had known her: but that one day lying negligently on her bed, a light appeared in her dark room, the brightness of which blinded her, and that it penetrated three times into her body, and that if she brought not three sons into the world she would submit to the most cruel torments. The three sons were born, and the princess was esteemed a saint."

This legend agrees in substance with the Immaculate Conceptions of Jesus and Buddha, and a similar story is told of Tamarlane the Earth-Shaker. When Genghis Khan was born the astrologers who were called pronounced that a Divine Man had come into the world, further testimony to which was the red stone which he clasped in his hand at birth. Thus this horoscope, if correct, may well be considered to represent the nativity of an Avatar.

According to Jacob Abbott, there was an old astrologer named Sujujin who was the principal minister and astrologer to Genghis Khan's father. This astrologer, also a distant relative of the chieftain, was the one who foretold that Genghis Khan would grow up to become a great warrior, conquering all his enemies, and extending his conquests to the most distant corners of the earth; in the end to become Khan of all Tartary. While Genghis was still a small child, the aged astrologer died and his son Karasher was appointed as the guardian and instructor of the future conqueror. Karasher trained the young chieftain in those arts and sciences which he deemed indispensable to the grand destiny which Sujujin the star-gazer had foretold for him.

An interesting fragment relating to the astrology of Genghis Khan is to be found in the *Outline History of China* by Herbert H. Gowen, F.R.G.S. In the midst of his conquests "the Mongol was impressed with unfavorable conjunctions of planets as with a presentiment of approaching doom. He set his face westward, but only reached the Sekaig in Kansu, when he was seized with illness. Shortly afterwards, at the camp in the Province of Shansi . . . Genghis Khan died at the age of 65." According to the directional astrology of Naibod, the Khan died at the square of the progressed Uranus to the Moon, at which time Neptune, by progression, also formed an opposition to the Moon from the tenth house.

Kublai Khan, the grandson of Genghis, was a great patron of science, literature and art. To him goes credit for several of the great astronomical instruments now preserved in the Observatory at Peking. He encouraged European priests and accepted Tibetan Buddhism, recognizing it as a useful instrument for the civilization of his people. On one occasion a revolt occurred in his kingdom, the greater part of the dissenting faction being Christian. Kublai, with fine strategy, surprised these revolutionists, captured and disarmed them, and caused them all, to the number of about fifteen thousand, to be brought into his presence, presumably to hear sentence of death. Seated upon the back of a great elephant, Kublai Khan called for silence and addressed the Christian prisoners in these words:

"Though I confess my great victory, this day gotten, was by the power and favor of my gods, the Sun, the Moon, and the stars, abiding in the glorious firmament of the heaven; yet because the prisoners, being all or most of them Christians, appear before me not only despoiled of their arms, but mocked and taunted of the Jews, Mohammedans and others, upbraiding them with their god Jesus, who was sometimes fastened unto a cross by the forefathers of these Jews: notwithstanding they have opposed me in battle, and that so many of their ensigns lie here prostrate at my feet; yet that all the nations and languages that live under our principality and dominion, may know, that we in our grace can find as soon will to pardon as power to punish; from this day forward, we forbid, and strictly charge all nations under us, of what quality or religion soever, that they neither deride, injure, or oppress any of these captive Christians, upon penalty to be deprived of their arms, and disgracefully scourged with rods. The main reason inducing us to see this exactly performed, being no other, but that their god Jesus is highly esteemed and honored by us as being one of the greatest among the celestial deities full of all equity and justice."[7]

[7] See Heywood's *Hierarchy of the Blessed Angels.*

# ASTROLOGY AND SCIENCE

*"I Confess that It Is Possible that the Motions of the Stars May Be Signs of Occurrences in the World, as the Lines of the Hands Are of Things in the Body."*—BARON GOTTFRIED WILHELM VON LEIBNITZ.

WHEN a scientific gentleman of letters is unfortunate enough to choose astrology as the subject for a literary endeavor, the result is unbelievably unscientific. In the preparation of this present work it has been our painful duty to peruse several of the latest "Outlines," "Criticisms," "Surveys," "Summaries," and "Remarks" relevant to the subjects of ancient and modern astrology. The commentaries of these learned critics are almost without exception monuments to the ignorance of their authors. It is to wonder by what perverted genius astronomers, mathematicians and physicists manage to accumulate between the covers of their literary productions such "mulligans" of misinformation.

Let us suppose for a moment that the biographies of great men were to be written by scientists. The following might be a neat, brief, and conservative treatise upon the subject, *Abraham Lincoln*: "Abraham Lincoln, class mammalia, species homo sapiens, was a body occupying place which integrated in 1809 and disintegrated in 1865. This body was presumably composed of approximately the following elements: Oxygen 65 percent, carbon 18 percent, hydrogen 10 percent, nitrogen 3 percent, calcium 2 percent, phosphorus 1 percent, the remaining 1 percent being made up of small quantities of potas-

94

sium, sodium, chlorine, magnesium, iron, iodine, fluorine, and silicon. The type is peculiar to the planet Earth."

This description of the Great Emancipator, though highly "scientific" and true to fact, nevertheless passes beyond the vanishing point of unimportance. The real Abraham Lincoln was an intellectual energy, a moral force, a courageous spirit, whose life and works profoundly influenced the course of civilization. Physicists might compute his specific gravity forever and yet never discover Abraham Lincoln, the *Man*.

In harmony with this viewpoint, we might hazard the speculation that astronomers have not yet "discovered" the intelligent universe. Though every element in cosmos be found and classified, the cosmos itself may still remain unknown. If astronomers say that Jupiter is a mass of gases, they but state a truth equally applicable to man. Yet the average savant would scarcely rejoice in such a definition of himself. He would rather insist that his molecules and atoms have conspired to create a genius.

It is quite scientific to presume that the universe bestowed all its intelligence upon man, leaving nothing but the mechanical qualities of rotation and revolution to be distributed among the suns, moons, and stars— that race of giants which populates the firmament? If human behavior is intelligent, why is not universal behavior also intelligent? If an insignificant mass of atoms on this earth could produce that Promethean soul of Abraham Lincoln, why should not a greater mass of atoms in the sky engender a still vaster spirit? If no evidence of divine intelligence can be discovered in the chemical composition of the stars, it may be said with equal truth that no evidence of human intelligence can be discovered in the chemical composition of man. The ancient pagan belief that the stars were the bodies of Great Beings replete with wisdom, who could be properly regarded as "divine," is no more unreasonable or inconsistent with science than to maintain that hydrogen and oxygen, together with thirteen other elements, when combined in the form of a college professor, are capable of propounding advanced problems in calculus.

If, then, astrology postulates the heavenly bodies to be foci of intellectual energy, it claims nothing more unreasonable for the stars than that which is evident in man himself. By his benevolence or despotism, a single man can change the moral temper of civilization. History has demonstrated that a man may have an influence far beyond that which would seem consistent with the measure of his stature or its physical displacement. Furthermore, this personal force will communicate itself to future generations and continue as a dynamic impulse long after the man himself has been dissipated. Likewise the sidereal bodies, as parts of a universal harmony or equilibrium, as factors in a balanced scheme, and as modes of behavior certainly constitute a heavenly environment, each contributing its physical ray to the rest and receiving into itself the moral electricity of brother spheres.

By destroying the sense of wholeness, analysis has the tendency to reduce all bodies to an insensate condition. Synthesis, on the other hand, by affirming wholeness and continually striving to envision such a state, tends to view all natures and forms as essentially sensate. If for the purpose of argument it be admitted that the structure of a planet renders it incapable of being an intellectual agent—a contention which certainly is not justified by fact—it still does not necessarily follow that even an insensate body is incapable of exerting a moral force. Music is an excellent example. For this art causes sounds—which feel no emotion in themselves (as far as known) and which certainly have no emotional organism such as that possessed by man—to produce the most intense reactions in the human soul.

The whole tendency of our present mind is from shallow prejudice to deeper fact. It may be interesting to trace the evolution of astrological belief through the opening years of our present century. For this purpose we shall have recourse to that "incomparable safeguard against misinformation"—the *Encyclopaedia Britannica*. The 9th edition of this revelation to the proletarian intellect defines astrology as "the *so-called* [italics mine, M. P. H.] science by which various nations, in various ways, have attempted to assign to the material heavens a moral influence over the earth and its inhabitants." With this appears also the following "requiem" to the general thought: "It is no longer necessary to protest against an error which is dead and buried."

Dr. J. H. Smith, in *The Arena,* gives the articles which appeared in the early editions of the *Encylopaedia Britannica* a thorough and well-justified castigation. To quote him: "The article on astrology—it might with more truth be said *against* astrology—in the *Encyclopaedia Britannica,* is often referred to, as having furnished the stroke of grace to an expiring superstition. The publishers, in disregard of a good custom, entrusted its preparation, not to a responsible and scholarly exponent of astrology, such as might easily have been found, even among the graduates of Oxford and Cambridge, but to one who dips his pen in venom at the start."

To that small circle of self-satisfied opinionists among whom criticism is a synonym for scholarship, the 14th and latest edition of the *Encyclopaedia Britannica* will prove less comforting. Astrology is herein defined as "the ancient art or science of divining the fate and future of human beings from indications given by the positions of the stars and other heavenly bodies." The *Encyclopaedia Britannica*—that "powerful instrument of education" which "helps you determine your standard of living"—turns apostate and defines astrology as a *science.* Nor is the word science qualified by *so-called, pseudo* or *quasi,* and, strange as it may appear, the word *superstition* does not occur even once in the opening sentence.

But that is not the worst. The commentary has also changed its tone. For example: "It is at least conceivable that some new analysis might once more justify part at all events of ancient and medieval astromancy, to the extent of admitting the empirical facts where provable, [sic!] and substituting for the supposed influence of the stars as such, some deeper theory which would be consistent with an application to other forms of prophecy, and thus might reconcile the possibility of dipping into futurity with certain interrelations of the universe, different indeed from those assumed by astrological theory, but underlying and explaining it." In other words, we may have all the astrological theories we want as long as the stars are not involved therein!

Radio has been a powerful factor in justifying astrology. It demonstrates the presence in Nature of an invisible sympathy susceptible of communication between visible bodies. It also reveals the existence of an electrical universe, each part of which receives into itself and distributes throughout its parts various modes of cosmic energy. It has recently been discovered that the moon has a distinct effect upon the radio. According to the McGraw-Hill Service Bureau: "As soon as the moon rises, reception falls off 50 per cent." The following explanation has been advanced: "Swinging through space, the moon collects negative electrostatic charges from electrons poured upon it by the sun, and the charged moon, passing over the earth's Heaviside layer, induces an electrostatic in it, thus affecting underlying layers and interfering with radio transmission, especially long-distance transmission."

Is it consistent with established learning to maintain that this "charged moon" affects nothing but the radio? Is not man himself an electrical mechanism, maintained by electrical energy, and fully as sensitive to vibrations as a radio receiving set? Reasonable answers to these two questions must inevitably constitute a case in favor of astrology, now regarded as one of the lowest forms of scientific heresy. But the astronomer will argue that this lunar phenomena can have no "moral" effect. Even here, however, his argument is weak; for morality is only an adaptation of energy, our codes being peculiar to our kind.

From Tucson, Arizona comes the interesting news that Dr. D. T. MacDougal, Director of the Laboratory, is to carry on experiments in an effort to discover the effect of the moon on planting and plant life. Although this has been abundantly examined and written upon by philosophers and scientists for the last five thousand years, Dr. MacDougal says that if the experiments demonstrate the validity of this idea, "it may be one of the most important discoveries ever made." (!!) Among the scientific it would seem that a "discovery" constitutes the acceptance by them of a well known and unquestioned fact.

Now comes a brand-new department of learning—the science of birthday influences. Of course, this has nothing to do with the stars but is the outcome of a systematic effort to discover what effect the seasons have upon the destiny of individuals. The result is definite evidence that winter and summer, with the conditions peculiar to each, are distinct factors in the production of genius. It has been discovered that December furnished more than its share of patients to a certain medical institution in Switzerland and that genius prefers to enter this world in February. It is admitted that the motion of the heavenly bodies determines the seasons. It is now being demonstrated that the seasons, in turn, have an effect upon mental ability. But our modern scientific men insist that it is not the stars but the food values and the weather that are responsible for it all. Or, is it *B. coli* which make us what we are today? It might prove embarrassing, however, to inquire further into the origin of either the food values or the weather, lest the stargazers of old score another victory.

A foreign criminologist published some years ago what he termed an Almanac of Crime, as the result of extensive research to determine the seasonal periodicity of various crimes. The following is an example of his findings:

"Murder—Many cases of this crime occur in August, January and June; few in February, November and December.

Infanticide—Dangerous periods are February and May; very few cases occur in September and December.

Poisoning—May is the favorite month for criminals of this type; during September as a rule they remain absolutely idle.

Threats of death—Many such threats are made in August and few in February, May and November.

Perjury—December and February are the two months during which this crime is most prevalent.

Forgery—During April, October and December forgers are most busy and also during the first days of every quarter and the last days of every year.

Theft—More crime of this kind are committed in December and January (winter months) than during any other months of the year."[11]

Dr. Charles Nordmann, a noted French savant, has discovered that X-rays of great intensity and undoubtedly of great effect upon the human organism emanate from the stars. "The action of the penetrating X-rays affects all atoms," says the good doctor, "particularly those of our body tissues. All our organs, the heart, nerves, blood and brain, therefore are being continually modified, but celestial X-rays coming from the stars, which abundantly emit these rays, exercise influence on the life organisms of each of us. . . . We therefore have a good reason to ask ourselves whether the stars emitting celestial rays, which act upon us incessantly, are not the cause of human cancer."[12]

The "unkindest cut of all" appears in *The Literary Digest* for March 12, 1932, where we learn that sun-spots, meddling in terrene affairs, cause variation "in the litters of rabbits and foxes." To quote the article: "One little sun-spot, barely visible to the naked eye, has been shown to radiate to the earth as much ultra-violet as all the rest of the sun's surface combined; and a few such spots occurring together obviously would produce a tremendous increase in the ultra-violet received on earth. It is this excess of ultra-violet, which upsets our radio in eleven-year cycles, by ionizing the Heaviside reflecting

---

[1] See *Star of the Magi*, Feb., 1902.
[2] See the *N. Y. Times*, Jan. 15th, 1927.

layer, giving us at present, wonderful long-distance reception and also badly chopped near-by fading of the broadcasting waves. Its effect also is shown strongly in the rings of all trees, which reveal the same somewhat irregular but average eleven-year periods of markings. Lake levels, grain crops, and even financial depressions seem to follow the same law. Each of the past four major depressions can be spotted about thirty months after a sun-spot maximum."

How a scientifically trained man can admit the possibility that ultra-violet rays from sun-spots can produce a financial panic and in the same breath brand astrology as nothing better than a superstition of the ancients is striking testimony to the inconsistency of our higher education. If the sun-spot can interpret itself in terms of crops, rabbit's fur, and tree rings, why should it leave no mark upon the moral life of man when, according to our prominent materialists, morality itself is merely a "stupid" behavior of electrons?

# ASTROLOGY AS A RELIGION

*"One Sees in the First Decan of the Sign Virgo, According to the Most Ancient Traditions of the Persians, Chaldeans, Egyptians, of Hermes, and of Aesculapius, a Young Woman Called in the Persian Language* SECLENIDOS DE DARZAMA, *a Name Translated Into the Arabian Tongue by* ADRENADEFA—*that is to Say, a Chaste, Pure, Immaculate Virgin, of a Beautiful Figure and an Agreeable Face, Having an Air of Modesty, Wearing Long Hair, Holding in Her Hand Two Ears of Corn, Seated on a Throne, Nourishing and Suckling a Young Child, Whom Some Call* JESUS, *and Whom We Call in Greek the* CHRIST."—ALBUMAZAR.

THE subject of astrology is susceptible of classification under three general headings. The religious aspect of astrology should properly be termed *astrolatry;* the scientific aspect, *astromancy.* It is generally admitted that the Chaldeans and other early nations derived their religious doctrines largely from their observations of the heavenly bodies and their seasonal effect upon terrestrial affairs. One writer has said: "That in the earth's earlier stages, man deduced his religion from his celestial surroundings and, observing the stars in their courses, worked out a scheme which has come down almost intact to us through sixty centuries, is well established."[1] It is erroneous to suppose that modern religions have departed greatly from the older doctrines, for the legends of pagan gods and Christian saints are equally founded upon the courses of the stars. Albertus Magnus wrote of Jesus that "all the mysteries of His divine incarnation, and all the secrets of His wonderful life, from His conception to His ascension, are to be found in the

[1] Edgar Lee.

103

constellations, and figured in the stars that announced them." That the Catholic Church recognized its own religious beliefs to be fundamentally astronomical is plainly evident from the following: "In the time of Leo I, some of the Fathers of the Church said that 'what rendered the festival (of Christmas) venerable was less the birth of Jesus Christ than the return, and, as they expressed it, the new birth of the sun.' "[2] Leo I, surnamed the Great, occupied the Holy See, from 440 to 461 A. D. The proximity of this period to the church's inception adds greatly to the significance of the statement.

The religions of the ancients were philosophies rather than systems of theological disputation. The temples were also the universities and it was not until the decay of classical antiquity that the divine aspects of learning came to be ignored. From a study of the heavens, therefore, it is possible to reconstruct the systems of belief that dominated earlier civilizations and which, later corrupted, resulted in the confusion worse confounded with which ecclesiasticism must now contend. "The pure practice of celestial philosophy," writes Alfred J. Pearce, "in course of time became corrupted into the worship of the heavens, or Zabaism, and afterwards into idolatry, or the worship of images found to resemble certain qualities of the planets in honor of which they were instituted. At first, men began to attribute the effects, which they perceived were produced by the celestial bodies, to the powers of those bodies as gods or demons of an inferior rank to the great FIRST CAUSE, whose majesty was gradually lost sight of to some extent. It has been doubted by some writers whether the ancient gods were named from the planets. This doubt could only arise in the minds of those persons who have only examined

2 See Mankind: Their Origin and Destiny.

the writings of the poets of Greece and Rome. It is dispelled by a proper study of the mythology of the ancient inhabitants of India, Phoenicia, and Egypt."[3]

Throughout antiquity the schools of heavenly Mysteries existed in every great civilized nation. The constellations and planets visible in the midnight sky were represented upon earth by shrines and temples of philosophic learning—schools of an inner wisdom. There were consequently twelve great Mysteries, all deriving their authority from the zodiacal hierarchies from which they flowed. The rites of Aries, or the Celestial Ram, were celebrated in the temple of Jupiter Ammon in the Libyan desert; the rites of Taurus in the Egyptian Mysteries of Serapis, or the tomb of the Heavenly Bull; the rites of Gemini in Samothrace, where Castor and Pollux —the Dioscuri—were hymned with appropriate ceremonial; the rites of Cancer in Ephesus, where Diana, the Multimammia, was revered; the rites of Leo in the Bacchic and Dionysiac orgies of the Greeks; the rites of Virgo by the Eleusinian Mysteries in Attica and the Christian rituals of the Virgin Mary. In India, Virgo is "Durga," a goddess of great power and dignity. The rites of Libra are peculiarly related to the Roman Catholic Church and the hieroglyph of Libra is worn as one of the chief ornaments of the Pope. The rites of the Scorpion are the Mysteries of the Apocalypse and the ceremonials of the Sabazians. The rites of Sagittarius are the Mysteries of the Centaurs. Chiron, one of this vanished race, was the mentor of Achilles. The rites of Sagittarius were of Atlantean origin, for Poseidon, the lord of the sea, was also the patron of the horse. The rites of Capricorn were the Mysteries peculiar to the Babylonians, and the composite body of the sea-goat signifies that

[3] See *Text-book of Astrology.*

these were celebrated at the twin cities of Babylon and Nineveh. The rites of Aquarius, the ancient water-man, pertain to the Mysteries of Ganymede, the cupbearer of Zeus and the lord of the ethers—keeper of those waters which are between the heavens and the earth. The rituals of the Holy Grail are also inferred. The rites of Pisces are those of the fish-gods, Oannes and Dagon; for, as St. Augustine writes: "There is a sacred fish which was broiled and eaten by the sinful for the redemption of their souls." Pisces is also the sign of the great Deluge, when the waters of heaven, descending upon the earth, mark the close of a Kalpa, or cycle of manifestation, when the worlds cease and the Creator upon His serpent couch floats over the surface of oblivion.

The planets were venerated in like manner, and the Seven Wonders of the ancient world were erected by Initiate Builders as monuments to the sky wanderers. The Colossus of Rhodes was an altar to the sun, the temple of Diana at Ephesus to the moon, the Great Pyramid to Hermes, or Mercury, the hanging gardens of Semiramis to Venus, the mausoleum of Halicarnassus to Mars, Olympian Zeus to Jupiter, and the Pharos of Alexandria to Saturn. The medieval Cabalists made much of these analogies, declaring them to evidence the universal diffusion of the Heavenly Mysteries. Thus while the origin of man's concept of the planets and zodiacal constellations, together with the forms which he assigns to them, must remain an unsolved mystery, the doctrines founded upon the orders of the stars and the wanderings of the planets through the houses of heaven have come to dominate in a most powerful way the affairs of men. The ancient astrologers were wiser than their modern imitators, for they were in possession of a secret doctrine relating to the Mysteries of the constellations.

If this doctrine could be re-established, it would go far to clarify the all-too-complicated issues of modern life, as well as re-elevate astrology to its true position of dignity as the cornerstone of the house of human learning. Pagan and Christian alike are united by astrology, for all faiths—with the possible exception of a few primitive forms—are astrological in origin. This fact alone should develop tolerance in matters of religion and incline us to study the sacred science of the stars and learn the import of their respective revelations.

The myths of ancient nations may often be interpreted with the aid of certain astrological keys. Saturn is sometimes referred to in the fables as an ass, Jupiter as an eagle, Mars as a wolf, the Sun as a lion, Venus as a dove, Mercury as a dragon, and the Moon as an ox. In the same way the Pleiades were called "the Doves," and Hydra was a name for the dragon-spirited Mercury in the sign of Virgo.[4] We can thus better understand what was inferred by Origen when he said: "In Egypt the philosophers have a sublime and secret knowledge respecting the nature of God, which they only disclose to the people under a cover of fables or allegories." The eight gods of Zenocrates are the five planets, the sun, the moon, and the firmament.

World religions are profoundly influenced by the precession of the equinoxes, which results in the yearly birth of the sun taking place in a new zodiacal sign every 2,160 years. According to the astronomical religion of the ancients, the annual incarnation of the sun was said to take place in a form or body corresponding to the zodiacal constellation which the sun occupied at the vernal equinox, i.e. the point of its crossing (or "passover") from the southern to the northern hemisphere. Pearce

[4] See *Mankind: Their Origin and Destiny.*

believes, for instance, that Buddha actually represents
the solar power ministering to the world in that age
when the vernal equinox took place in Gemini. Mercury is the ruler of Gemini; therefore, the sun in its
equinoctial splendor takes upon itself the form of this
"just man" and through him reveals the Law. "The
struggle between *Buddha* (Mercury) and *Mara* (Mars)
is in strict harmony with astrological principles, for Mars
is always at enmity with Mercury; and the victory
achieved by Buddha over worldly allurements and the
'terrible array' of Mara's hosts, is singularly suggestive
of the triumph of our Savior over Satan."[5]

Later when the vernal equinox occurred in the constellation of Taurus, it was declared that the Bull of the
year broke the annual egg with his horns. Osiris was the
Sun-God, and when he took upon himself the form of
the Celestial Bull he was declared to have been born in
the body of that beast. For this reason, when the astrologers erected the annual horoscope of Egypt, they chose
the moment of this incarnation, ascertaining therefrom
the pleasure of the god. In India, the god Shiva rides
upon the great white bull, Nandi, and the children of
Israel made offerings to a golden calf because they were
released from Egypt in the age of the Bull.

In the Cabirian rites, the initiates stood under spe-
cially prepared sacrificial gratings and were bathed in
the blood of sacred bulls. In the Eleusinian and Bacchic
rites, candidates took their vows of secrecy while standing upon the skins of newly sacrificed bulls. In the Mithraic Mysteries, Mithras—the solar Savior-God—is
depicted driving his sword into the heart of a bull to remind the initiated philosopher that the vital force by
which Nature is maintained is mystically the blood of

5 See *The Text-book of Astrology.*

Taurus. The University of Oxford derives its names from the Celestial Ox, because of the Mithraic and Druidic figures of this animal discovered in the environs of the college. It is also assumed that the bleeding heart, so conspicuous among the symbols of Roman Catholicism, was originally the heart of an ox, but when through the precession of the equinoxes the lamb came to the angle, the heart of this creature was substituted for that of the bull.

In that age during which the vernal equinox occurred in Aries, the solar divinity was represented as a golden-haired youth holding in one hand a lamb and in the other a shepherd's crook. Thousands of years before the birth of Christ, the pagans adored this figure of life and beauty. On the day of the equinox they gathered in the squares before their temples, crying out as with a single voice: "All hail, Lamb of God, which taketh away the sin of the world!" Jupiter Ammon is depicted with rams' horns upon his forehead, and the Moses of Michelangelo is similarly adorned. Jupiter Pan, or Lord of the World —the symbol of the generating power of the sun—was represented as a goat-man. In Greek mysticism, the Golden Fleece is directly related to the ritualism of Aries. This fleece is "the wool of the wise," the same wool which they pull over the eyes of the foolish. According to Zadkiel, "In Aries the Sun was called *Chrisna,* from which, probably, the Greeks formed their *Krios,* a ram, from the Chaldee, *Kresa,* a throne, or seat of power; in allusion to the power of the Sun when in Aries, his exaltation."

After passing 2,160 years in the sign of the Ram, the heavenly rotations caused the vernal equinox to take place in Pisces, and during that period "the Light of the World" appeared as the Fisher of Men." The world has just passed through the Piscean cycle, which by the very nature of the sign has been an age of travail, for Pisces is the last zodiacal sign and is the sidereal instrument of retribution. The new Aquarian Age which is to come is the age of mysticism and invention, the era of the heavenly water, when the god of the world shall appear clothed in an electrical garment, releasing his divine energies as a stream of stars from the urn of the Celestial Water-bearer.

# ASTROLOGY AS A PHILOSOPHY

*"The Body of a Man Is His House; the Architect Who Builds It Is the Astral World, the Carpenters Are at One Time Jupiter, at Another Venus; at One Time Taurus, at Another Orion. Man Is a Sun and a Moon and a Heaven Filled with Stars; the World Is a Man, and the Light of the Sun and the Stars Is His Body; the Ethereal Body Cannot Be Grasped, and Yet It is Substantial, Because Substance Means Existence, and Without Substance Nothing Exists."*—PARACELSUS.

ASTROLOGY may also be defined as the philosophy of discovering and analyzing past impulses and future actions of both individuals and nations by the positions, motions, and configurations of the heavenly bodies. It, furthermore, maintains that the life of an individual or the duration of a circumstance is subject—at least, in its generalities—to the planetary influences that were focussed upon the place of its beginning at the moment of its inception. It follows that if two persons were born in the same place at the same time, they would be subject to the same destiny, which destiny, however, would be qualified by the social environment into which they were ushered at birth. For this reason, astrology is also the science of estimating the effect of qualities upon temperaments and conditions. Of course, unbelievers scoff at such a possibility, and it is rare that the opportunity is afforded to demonstrate the astrologer's premises, for even in the case of so-called identical twins a few moments elapse between the delivery of the two children. English records preserve the details of an extraordinary circumstance by which the contention of astrologers is

111

sustained. The "doubting Thomas" is invited to explain this matter to his own satisfaction.

On the 4th day of June, 1738, in the parish of St. Martins-in-the-Fields, at almost identically the same minute, two boys were born into this world. One was William Frederick, later crowned George the Third, King of England. The other was James Hemming, who was to become a distinguished and industrious member of the Iron Mongers' Guild. Widely separated in physical estate yet bound by astral influences to parallel destinies, these two men, each in his own social sphere, lived out the edict of his stars. In October, 1760, when George the Third came to the throne, thereby fulfilling the purpose for which he was born, John Hemming went into business for himself, thus accomplishing the height of his ambition. Both men were married on the 8th day of September, 1761, and it is interesting to note that there was a startling similarity in appearance between the king and the ironmonger. In the newspapers of February, 1820, were conspicuous notices of the passing of His Majesty, the King, and in the same newspapers was the obscure obituary notice of John Hemming, ironmonger. Both men died on Saturday, January 29th, according to the best records available, within less than an hour of each other.

To defend his science and himself, the astrologer must be prepared to deal with two objections which are almost certain to rise in the minds of the uninformed. In the first place, astrologers are accused of promoting the theory of fatalism; in the second place, it has been asserted that predictions—especially of an unfortunate nature—have a demoralizing effect upon the mind, resulting in disastrous psychological reactions or complexes. Both of these objections, however, are referable not to the actual doctrines of astrology but rather to a misunderstanding thereof. The ablest men of all races and times have consulted their stars, nor were their minds adversely affected thereby. The reason may be unseated by an unbalanced addiction to almost any pursuit, but where the intellect is inherently sound, astrology will rather increase than diminish its efficiency. An astrologer well grounded in his science will, if he possesses the capacity therefor, be the most reasonable and rational of men, enriched rather than impoverished by his devotion to the heavenly lore.

Fatalism finds no justification in the doctrines of the early astrologers. "There is no fatal necessity in the stars," wrote Lord Bacon, "and this, the more prudent astrologers have constantly allowed." Claudius Ptolemy, astrologer *emeritus,* was in no respect a fatalist, for in his *Centiloquy,* he gives this aphorism: "A skillful person, acquainted with the nature of the stars, is enabled to avert many of their effects and to prepare himself for those effects before they arrive." The ancient masters of the starry science taught that to be forewarned is to be forearmed. This is common sense rather than predestination. A few references relevant to this subject are taken from the writings of the learned Franciscan monk, Roger Bacon: "It is not Ptolemy's thought that the astrologer should give any particular and fixed judgment and one sufficing in individual cases: but that his judgment should be a general one and a mean between what is necessary and what is impossible, and the astrologer is not able in all cases to give a final judgment." He further says: "The rational soul is able to change greatly and impede the effects of the stars, as in the case of infirmities and pestilences of cold and heat, and famine, and in many other matters." And again: "Whence Isaac

says, 'Evil does not happen to a man unless he is re-
strained by ignorance of the celestial science.' " Later he
adds: "From these statements, then, it is clear that philosophers do not maintain that there is an inevitable
happening of events in all cases due to celestial influences, nor is their judgment infallible in particular in-
stances." And to summarize: "True mathematicians and
astronomers or astrologers, who are philosophers, do not
assert a necessity and an infallible judgment in matters
contingent on the future. Therefore, any person attrib-
uting these erroneous views to these men are clearly
proved guilty of ignorance of philosophy, and reprobate
the truth of which they are ignorant."[1]

Philosophically speaking, that man who does not rule
himself is ruled by fate, even as a ship without a helms-
man is at the mercy of the sea. In this sense a wise man
is said to rule his stars, for destiny is perfected by "art"
—to borrow a Hermetic phrase. Through learning, man
is enabled to anticipate Nature in some matters; as, for
example, in the case of crops where, through skill, he
may considerably increase his harvest. Through familiarity with the heavenly science, the philosopher is deterred
from unwise action and by opportunely changing his
course may achieve to the best of the several destinies
which the heavens have indicated. Ptolemy therefore
affirms that the error of fatalism arises from failure to
note that in nearly every combination of planets several
testimonies are involved. That is, when a planet is
afflicted by one or more malignancies, at the same time
it nearly always enjoys benefic influences from some part
of the heavens. An astrologer who predicts only evil
speaks not for the stars but from some bias within himself, for the constellations are scarcely ever so conjoined

[1] See *Opus Majus.*

that their malevolence is not tempered by some kindly and redeeming force. A man who plunges headlong or blindly into some venture is more likely to come under the despotism of fatality than one who reasons and analyzes. If we permit ourselves to come into violent contact with certain natural laws, we destroy our power of choice, or free-will, as some call it. Under such conditions, destiny becomes inevitable. If a man jumps off a cliff, he is destined to fall. Before the leap, he has the power of choice; but afterwards he is the victim of inevitable fate. Free-will leaves off where foolishness begins. Astrology may not deflect a madman from his purpose, but it can direct a wise man to the fullest expression of his power and ability. Astrology teaches neither fate nor free-will, but recognizes the law of cause and of Nature.

As to the second objection that "A belief in astrology has the most unfortunate tendency as to the morality of man" by leaving him a victim to either despair or absurd hope, this again is an unreasonable charge. Although astrologers untrained in the principles of the science may occasionally be guilty of such ethical impropriety, the science itself should not be discredited thereby. A person usually consults an astrologer because of some pressing difficulty. He is in trouble, has been in trouble, or is anticipating trouble. Many a sick man has been frightened to death by his physician, but an intelligent individual, discovering sickness in his body, is thankful for the information and takes immediate steps to master the infirmity. The astrologer is a counsellor who, warning his client of impending disaster, assists him to meet or circumvent the evil, as the case may be. A man who is not strong enough to face a fact is already demoralized. "It would be childish, therefore," writes

B. Suryanarain Row, "to talk of astrology as leading to fatalistic inactivity. Cowards were never crowned and they never benefited mankind."[2] Astrology only paralyzes initiative in an individual in whom such paralysis is constitutional. Astrology is only an excuse for weakness in those who are themselves weak. Nor do wise men hitch their wagons to stars. They rather observe the mutations caused in human affairs by the celestial agencies and adjust themselves easily to every new circumstance, thus living in unbroken tranquillity and dying with good hope.

There is another indictment against astrology not to be ignored. In time of war or other major catastrophes when thousands or even millions meet a common fate at nearly the same time, do the horoscopes of all these persons testify to such a common end or does some larger issue overweigh the testimony of the individual horoscope? Here again, however, a careful examination reveals that Nature does not contradict herself. The stars do not promise long life and then retract their boon. Nor is this fatalism, for though many may perish, individuality is preserved to the end. In war "some died of wounds by sword, others by shot, others by fire, water, falls, being crushed, blown up by gunpowder, etc." The same is true of earthquakes. "At the great earthquake at Lisbon, numbers were swallowed up, some drowned, some maimed, some burned; some died instantly, some lingered for weeks and months. Again, in wrecks, some are drowned, some are suffocated, or killed by blows, according to their several nativities."[3] In these same catastrophes there are others who come through unhurt, bearing, as it were, charmed lives.

[2] See *Introduction to Astrology*.
[3] See Cooke's *A Plea for Urania*.

Only one deeply skilled may perceive all these things from the horoscope, but science cannot advance any objections to astrology for which the astrologer cannot give a satisfactory explanation. If anyone should ask, is this not, then, fatalism and did not destiny gather these diversified careers to one place only to bring about their ruin? we would answer, Fate controls only those who, having no knowledge of it, move blindly to their own destruction. It was not destiny but ignorance of destiny that resulted in the tragedy. Astrology not only warns of that which is to occur but also makes those who are proficient in its mysteries the masters of their fate and captains of their souls. Through the use of astrology a wise man is enabled to avoid such mutations of fortune as are avoidable, and meet such ripe destiny as is un-avoidable with vision and fortitude.

In the fifteenth century there lived a man, Picus, Earl of Mirandola, who was called a prodigy of learning, for when but twenty-four years of age he had published eight hundred propositions in logic, mathematics, phys-ics, divinity, and the Kabbala. In this single personality all the opponents of astrology are epitomized. The Earl had such a violent antipathy to the starry science that he became known as the "scourge of astrology." Unwit-tingly, however, he was to become the outstanding proof of the accuracy of this imperishable art. Three different astrologers prophesied that this doughty nobleman would not live beyond his thirty-third year. Mirandola considered this prophecy a powerful weapon in his hands, for by it he would prove conclusively that the "star-mongers," as he called them, were knaves and dotards. But Picus spent so much time in criticism that he had none left in which to regulate the concerns of his life. Like other foolish mortals, he used his mind to condemn and not to think, and lo, and behold, on the very day—yes, the very hour that had been predicted —Mirandola died, thus championing the very cause he had sought to undo. Thus those who criticize astrology are themselves victimized by fate, while those sages whose reasoning they condemn escape outrageous circumstance and of all men alone enjoy freedom of will.

In *The British Journal of Astrology* appears the following tribute by James Harvey: "The greatest testimony to the truth of astrology is that it has never halted, but has come undeviatingly down through the ages, down out of the mist of time through the ancient world and the mediaeval night of horror, persecution, faggot and blood; from the prehistoric and ancient plains of Chaldea and Assyria here to our present time."

# ASTROLOGY'S PLACE IN THE
# MODERN WORLD

*"It Is but Fair to Admit, Further, That Astrology in the Hands of Its Best Exponents, Is Not Lacking in Dignity. If Our Lives Are to Be Governed by Anything in Nature, We Prefer to Have Them Governed by the Starry Host; in Fact, a Few of Us Would Prefer the Planets to Some of the Majorities Which Obtain in the House of Commons."*—T. SHARPER KNOWLSON.

HAVING traced the story of astrology through the vicissitudes of over forty centuries, it is appropriate that this essay should be concluded with a brief summary of the place occupied by the ancient science in more recent times. A critical reader, having examined the preceding pages, can legitimately advance but one more criticism. He may say, "But all this is ancient history and can have no bearing upon the affairs of this more enlightened (?) age." While it is true that astrology is seldom publicized in high places in our day, it is for the reason that ambitious mortals fear criticism which might impede the furtherance of their careers. But many of our greatest and most powerful have found it convenient, even comforting, to consult their stars. The more powerful a man becomes, the more forcibly he is impressed with his own weakness and insufficiency. Faced with numerous and weighty responsibilities and well aware of the fickleness of fortune, it is not superstition but experience which forces upon him the recognition of an administrative Providence. As Samuel Johnson, the eminent English literateur, so wisely observed, "The way to be happy is to live according to nature, in obedience to that universal and unalterable law with which every heart is originally impressed; which is not written on it by precept, but engraven by destiny, not instilled by education, but infused at our nativity."[1]

It might be appropriate to begin this section with a few words concerning the part that astrology played in the formation of the American nation. After observing that the horoscope of the United States has all the appearance of an electional figure,[2] Sir John Hazelrigg states definitely that "not a few" of those illustrious patriots who drafted the Declaration of Independence "were versed in the tenets of astrology." He continues, "this statement is warranted by annotations on the margins of the astrological books in the Thomas Jefferson Library (now in the Library of Congress); Franklin was a self-confessed votary, confirmed by his scientific delving and his *Poor Richard's Almanac;* and one cannot read Thomas Paine's *Age of Reason* without being convinced of his conversancy with the principles of astro-science and its philosophy. Other Signers could be included is this numeration . . .," etc., etc.[3]

Benjamin Franklin, scientist, philosopher, diplomat, Free-mason, astrologer and founder of the Saturday Evening Post, has well been titled the "first American gentleman." Dr. Franklin published a series of almanacs under the pseudonym of Richard Saunders, or Poor Richard. He borrowed this name from a distinguished astrologer-physician of the preceding century whose

[1] See *Rasselas.*

[2] An electional figure is a horoscope erected beforehand and used to calculate a propitious time for the beginning of some important event.

[3] See *Mercury:* Article: Our National Birthday.

great textbook on medical astrology published in 1677 contained an introduction by the most celebrated of the English astrologers, William Lilly. In his almanac for 1733 Benjamin Franklin makes the following prediction of the death of his friend and "fellow student" Mr. Titan Leeds: "He dies by my calculation made at his request, on October 17, 1733, 3 hours 29 minutes P. M. at the very instant of the conjunction of the Sun and Mercury."[4] Thus America's first Ambassador to France did not hesitate to acknowledge that he communed with the Uranian Muse. This published statement by the great American patriot can leave not the slightest doubt or question of Franklin's attitude towards astrology. When we compare this notable Philadelphian with some of our more recent politicians, we wonder whether it would not be wise to make astrology compulsory for diplomats.

Nor should we pass on to other times without mention of the researches of Robert Campbell whose exceedingly rare little book *Our Flag* shows that the flag of the United States was actually patterned by a man who was not only well versed in astrology but who, in the presence of Washington and Franklin, described the symbolism of the flag and the nation which it represented in terms of astrology and the zodiac.

No name stands out in the recent history of this country more forcibly than that of Theodore Roosevelt, twenty-sixth president of the United States. The immortal "Teddy," whose smile made a multitude of friends and whose big stick made political history, seems to have had more than a passing interest in the stars—especially his own stars. In this regard we quote

[4] See *National Astrological Journal:* Article: Benjamin Franklin, by Ralph Kraum.

three paragraphs from an article *Roosevelt and Astro-Science* by Jane C. Hunter:

"Mr. Dudley Clarke, traveler and author of many books on Masonic and Biblical symbolism, informed the writer that he had known Colonel Roosevelt personally, and had discust his birth-chart with him upon several occasions. Mr. Clarke stated that the Colonel had informed him that his father was a believer in the ancient science to the extent that he had the horoscope of the future president of the United States constructed by the father of Li Hung Chang, the Chinese statesman and general, when his young son and heir was just ten hours old.

"Upon one occasion when Mr. Clarke reminded Colonel Roosevelt that he had some rather disconcerting squares in his chart, the Colonel laughingly waved these aside with the remark that he intended to live by his sextile and trine, Venus-Jupiter to his M. C. True, even then, however, to his oft-voiced principle in later years, viz: 'Trust God, but keep your powder dry,' the Colonel confided to Mr. Clarke that he always kept his weather-eye on the opposition of the Moon in his seventh house to Mars in his first.

"Mr. Clarke stated that Colonel Roosevelt himself enlarged and etched his natal figure on some durable material, and had mounted it on a chess-board which always stood on a table in his room, and that when the Colonel was contemplating some momentous undertaking he would estimate the facility with which it would be accomplisht, or the difficulties attending its consummation, by his ability to quickly checkmate the Queen, which represented the Moon opposing Mars in his horoscope."[5]

[5] See *Mercury*, Sept., 1930.

It will be noted that the quotation also mentions the great Chinese statesman the Earl Li Hung Chang, the most powerful figure in the modern history of Cathay. When we realize that Li Hung Chang was born under a conjunction of Neptune and Uranus and that in his chart, Mars, Venus and Mercury are conjunct in Pisces, and the Moon and Saturn are conjunct in Taurus, with an exact square of Jupiter and the Sun, we can better appreciate the genius of the man whose stupendous intellectual equipment, however, was unable to completely offset the uncertain fortunes indicated by Jupiter's affliction. Li Hung Chang once said, with a slight smile, to Prince Bismarck, "They call me the Bismarck of China," whereupon the Prince instantly replied, with evidence of great admiration, "But they will never call me the Li Hung Chang of Germany." The governor of a large Chinese city once observed that Li Hung Chang was born the year Napoleon died because "nature abhorred a vacuum." A more wily diplomat or crafty statesman than Li Hung Chang never outwitted the politicians of Europe. Who knows, possibly he had an astrological advantage and knew how to use it.

From the time of the astrologer who compared the horoscopes of Napoleon and Wellington, declaring that if ever the Englishman met the Frenchman in battle Napoleon would lose, astrology has occupied a quiet but dignified position in the mundane matters of war and policy. The German government solicited the assistance of the English astrologer Raphael in the choosing of a propitious time for the commencement of the Franco-Prussian War. When Bismarck and von Moltke were enjoying carte blanche at Versaille, Raphael received a present of one hundred pounds from the Germans "in appreciation" of the accuracy of the advice

which he had given and the successful campaign which
had resulted from starting their offensive under favorable planetary configurations.

The significance of an electional figure may be better
understood if we observe that the unfortunate ships the
Titanic and the Lusitania and the equally unhappy dirigibles the Shenandoah and the Akron were all launched
under extremely unfavorable planetary positions. Flamsteed chose a propitious electional figure for the dedication of Greenwich Observatory, and the dignity and
success of this institution, which has become the center
of practically all nautical and astronomical calculation,
bears witness to the wisdom of his choice and the power
of the stars.

We are indebted to Llewellyn George for the research
which gives up the following valuable data:

"Here is another instance concerning the use of Judicial Astrology: The Japanese are very proficient in
this branch, and, in connection with their war against
Russia, while generals and statesmen everywhere were
predicting success for the Russian arms, Astrologers
unanimously declared that the Japs would be successful.
The Japanese themselves, through their knowledge of
Astrology, never sought a battle except on a day that
would be good for them and bad for the Russians, with
the result that they were astoundingly victorious in
spite of superior forces."

Count Hamon, better known as Cheiro, was the most
famous contemporary exponent of divinatory arts. In a
recent series of articles Cheiro lists a number of celebrated men and women whose belief and interest in
astrology led them to consult him, seeking advice and
help from their horoscopes. Cheiro describes Admiral
George Dewey and General Nelson A. Miles as firm

believers in astrology; he describes President and Mrs. Grover Cleveland as keen believers in the planetary influences, and accurately predicted for Mrs. Cleveland the birth of her child. He then tells that it was largely through the influence of H.R.H. the Prince of Wales, later King Edward VII, that he gained his reputation as a seer. He was requested by the Czar of all the Russians to calculate the horoscopes of the members of the royal family and predicted accurately the fall of the house of Romanoff. He was visited by Leopold II, King of the Belgians, and was requested to make astrological calculations for him. He predicted a disaster at sea for Lord Kitchener in the 66th year of the Earl's life. He read the future of Sarah Bernhardt, and from the horoscope of Mata Hari predicted a violent death in 1917. These are but a few of the amazing list of celebrities whose belief in astrology caused them to turn to their horoscopes for guidance through the perplexing crises of their careers.[6]

In passing we cannot refrain from mentioning a curious belief held by Mark Twain. A New York newspaper some years ago published an interesting fragment from the life of America's beloved humorist. Mark Twain said that he was born with Halley's Comet and expected to die upon its return, and his death came exactly as he had predicted.

Ignominious indeed was the end of the glittering Turkish Sultanate. Abdul Hamid, surnamed the Damned, had failed to hear the voice of Allah in the rebellious utterances of his own people. F. G. Aflafo gives a dramatic picture of the last days of the old regime:

"What an inspiration some great historic-painter

[6] See *Confessions of a Modern Seer.*

might have drawn from these last furtive council meetings at Yildiz, held in dead of night and with closed doors. There sat the old autocrat, cornered at last like a boar in his lair, and around him his fawning courtiers, only one of whom dared tò breathe the forbidden word 'Constitution,' and he, an aged astrologer, whom, true to a life long hankering after the occult sciences, Abdul Hamid held in reverence."⁷

The outstanding exponent of astrology in twentieth century America was the late Evangeline Adams, a descendant of John Quincy Adams, sixth president of the United States. Evangeline Adams successfully defended astrology before the courts of this country, and at the end of the case the judge said, "The defendant raises astrology to the dignity of an exact science. Every fortune teller is a violator of the law but every astrologer is not a fortune teller."

To Miss Adams' studios in Carnegie Hall, New York, flocked the humble and the great. King Edward VII, Enrico Caruso, John Burroughs, Lillian Nordica, Geraldine Farrar and Mary Pickford were among her clients. To quote the *New York World:* Business men came too; even J. Pierpont Morgan [Sr.] and two former presidents of the N. Y. Stock Exchange, Seymour Cromwell and Jacob Stout. 'I read Mr. Morgan's horoscope many times,' Miss Adams said not long ago. 'He was skeptical at first. But I convinced him. During the last years of his life I furnished him a regular service. It explained the general effects of the planets on politics, business and the stock market.' "⁸

From these examples chosen at randon from a formidable array of facts, the force of astrology upon

⁷ See *Regilding the Crescent.*
⁸ Friday, Nov. 11th, 1932.

modern affairs can be somewhat adequately estimated. One more example must bring our writing to a close. There is no question but that Italy's Mussolini will go down in history as the real pioneer in the technique of dictatorship. *Le Matin,* the French newspaper, in its issue of May 9, 1923 contains the following thought-provoking paragraph:

"Just as Wallenstein consulted Zeno, who professed to read the stars, so does Signor Mussolini, every time he passes through Milan, go to visit a certain man named Rosconi, who is known in that city as Signor Mussolini's astrologer. This good man found his vocation as an astrologer when a simple soldier in 1918, and he predicted that the war would end in November of that year, neither before nor after. They tried to shut him up in a mad asylum but by chance he escaped this sad fate. Rosconi believes firmly in the science of astrology. As regards his actual predictions, the most surprising one is that another war will break out in ten years. Rosconi refuses to reveal the belligerents; all he will consent to say is that on this occasion Italy will annex some new territories."[9]

Thus we see that from the Namar-Beli composed by King Sargon I in the 3rd Millenium B. C.—the oldest known astrological document extant—to this very present day astrology has constantly contributed to the progress of empire and the civilization of the human race. It has not only kept faith with man, it has kept pace with progress. As it inspired antiquity, so it inspires the modern world. It lifts the human mind from the morbidity of imminent limitation; it gives order and perspective to all the complexities of life, and when wisely administered by a competent exponent is the most

[9] See *British Astrological Journal.*

useful and practical science which human inspiration and ingenuity has conceived.

The actual beginnings of astrology are unknown and unknowable. The science emerges already highly refined from the utter obscurity of the pre-historic world. The ends of astrology are also unknown. There is already evidence that the perfection of this science will elevate man to an intellectual and social condition far beyond the limitations of our present consciousness.

**COSIMO** is an innovative publisher of books and publications that inspire, inform and engage readers worldwide. Our titles are drawn from a range of subjects including health, business, philosophy, history, science and sacred texts. We specialize in using print-on-demand technology (POD), making it possible to publish books for both general and specialized audiences and to keep books in print indefinitely. With POD technology new titles can reach their audiences faster and more efficiently than with traditional publishing.

> ➢ **Permanent Availability:** Our books & publications never go out-of-print.

> ➢ **Global Availability:** Our books are always available online at popular retailers and can be ordered from your favorite local bookstore.

**COSIMO CLASSICS** brings to life unique, rare, out-of-print classics representing subjects as diverse as *Alternative Health, Business and Economics, Eastern Philosophy, Personal Growth, Mythology, Philosophy, Sacred Texts, Science, Spirituality* and much more!

**COSIMO-on-DEMAND** publishes your books, publications and reports. If you are an Author, part of an Organization, or a Benefactor with a publishing project and would like to bring books back into print, publish new books fast and effectively, would like your publications, books, training guides, and conference reports to be made available to your members and wider audiences around the world, we can assist you with your publishing needs.

Visit our website at www.cosimobooks.com to learn more about Cosimo, browse our catalog, take part in surveys or campaigns, and sign-up for our newsletter.

And if you wish please drop us a line at info@cosimobooks.com. We look forward to hearing from you.